THE UNCOMPLICATED LLC GUIDE FOR BEGINNERS

SIMPLE & DETAILED TECHNIQUES TO FORM YOUR BUSINESS, MAXIMIZE PROFITS, UNDERSTAND LEGAL SAFEGUARDS, AND PROTECT YOUR ASSETS

ROBERT PORTUGAL

TABLE OF CONTENTS

INTRODUCTION

Every year, hundreds of thousands of individuals step into the entrepreneurial arena, filled with dreams and aspirations to carve out their slice of the business world. Yet, amidst these bustling beginnings, many ventures face unnecessary risks that could be mitigated with the proper legal structure. Let me share a striking fact: Businesses operating as sole proprietorships expose their owners to extensive personal liability, potentially jeopardizing personal assets in the face of business debts or legal disputes. This is where an LLC comes into play, providing a shield for your assets and offering a simplified tax regimen, giving you the security and peace of mind to focus on your business.

My name is Robert Portugal, and over the years, I have guided countless budding entrepreneurs through the maze of business formation, focusing mainly on the strategic benefits of limited liability companies (LLCs). With extensive experience in tax strategy, legal compliance, and small business advocacy, I have witnessed firsthand the transformative impact a well-structured LLC can have on protecting and fostering a business, inspiring you to see the potential of your own business.

This guide is crafted to peel back the layers of complexity surrounding the formation and management of LLCs. It's designed for the aspiring entrepreneur eager to turn a vision into a reality while ensuring your personal assets remain secure. Many shy away from LLCs, bogged down by myths of intricate paperwork, high costs, and opaque legal jargon. This book will dismantle these myths, showing how accessible and beneficial forming an LLC can be and empowering you to take control of your business's legal structure.

The structure of this guide is straightforward yet thorough. Starting with the basics of an LLC and why it is a superior choice for many businesses, we will move through the practical steps of setting up your own LLC. You'll find detailed chapters on financial planning, understanding and maximizing tax benefits, navigating legal protections, and even considering international expansion. Each section is packed with step-by-step instructions, real-life examples, and actionable advice to help you apply what you learn directly to your business endeavors.

What sets this guide apart is its focus on demystifying the perceived complexities of tax benefits and legal safeguards while maintaining a motivational tone, encouraging you to proceed with clarity and confidence. This book isn't just about forming an LLC—it's about setting a solid foundation for your business dreams.

As someone who has walked the challenging path of entrepreneurship, I understand the hurdles and high stakes involved. My goal is to empower you with knowledge, enabling you to make informed, strategic decisions that protect and propel your business. This book is more than a guide—it's a companion on your journey to business success.

Let's begin this journey together. With each page, you'll gain knowledge and the confidence to step boldly into business ownership, equipped with the tools to safeguard your hard-earned assets and achieve your entrepreneurial ambitions.

LAYING THE GROUNDWORK FOR YOUR LLC

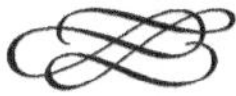

Did you know the first recorded LLC was formed in Wyoming in the late 1970s? It was a revolutionary concept at the time, designed to combine the best elements of corporations and partnerships. Fast forward to today, and LLCs have become the go-to structure for entrepreneurs who want the security of limited liability and the ease of a less formal business structure. But why has this particular business entity captured small business owners' hearts (and assets) across the country? Let's dive into the nuts and bolts of LLCs and explore how this could be a game-changer for your business aspirations.

1.1 WHAT IS AN LLC, AND WHY SHOULD YOU CHOOSE THIS STRUCTURE?

Definition and Basics

A limited liability company (LLC) is a hybrid business entity that encapsulates the flexibility of a partnership with the robust liability protection of a corporation. At its core, an LLC is designed to provide its owners, who are called members, protection from personal liability in most instances, which means personal assets are usually off-limits to business creditors. What sets it apart is its flexibility. Unlike the more rigid corporate structure that requires directors, officers, and shareholders, an LLC can be managed directly by its members or a designated manager.

Advantages of Choosing an LLC

One of the most enticing features of an LLC is pass-through taxation. This means the LLC itself does not pay taxes on business income. Instead, profits and losses are passed through to members' tax returns, sidestepping the double taxation bullet corporations often have to bite. This can lead to significant tax savings and simplify the tax filing process, making it an attractive option for many entrepreneurs.

Moreover, the protective shell of an LLC safeguards your assets, like your home, car, and savings, from business liabilities. This is a comforting assurance for anyone venturing into the business world, where uncertainties lie around every corner. Additionally, forming and maintaining an LLC is more convenient than doing so in a corporation. There are fewer record-keeping requirements, and the operational processes are generally less strict. This appeals to first-time business owners who might be intimidated by extensive bureaucratic red tape.

Entrepreneurial Attraction

The allure of LLCs particularly resonates with small business owners and solo entrepreneurs. The reason? Its simplicity and efficiency in setup and operation. Forming an LLC can be relatively straightforward, unlike other business entities that require hefty paperwork and complex setups. This simplicity is not just about ease but also about accessibility. It opens the doors to legal and financial security for less experienced individuals who might need more resources to navigate more complex structures.

Real-Life Examples

Consider the story of a small organic skincare shop that started as a humble home-based business. The owner decided to form an LLC, which protected her from personal financial risk and positioned the company as a credible entity in the market. This credibility helped attract more partnerships and larger contracts. Or take the example of a freelance graphic designer who transformed his freelance gigs into a full-fledged design studio under an LLC. This shift safeguarded his assets and provided a favorable tax treatment that enabled him to reinvest more into his business.

Both examples underscore how LLCs can serve as a springboard for small businesses, providing a structure that supports growth while minimizing risk. Whether you are crafting artisanal soaps in your kitchen or coding websites in a co-working space, the benefits of operating under an LLC can be substantial.

By understanding the foundational aspects of an LLC and why it might be the right choice for your business, you're better equipped to make informed decisions that align with your entrepreneurial goals and personal risk tolerance. As we explore the nuances of LLCs in the following sections, keep these advantages in mind—they might be the leverage you need to transform your business ideas into a sustainable, protected, and thriving enterprise.

1.2 DECODING LIMITED LIABILITY: HOW IT PROTECTS YOU AND YOUR ASSETS

Let's face it: "limited liability" sounds like something you'd hear in a particularly dry legal seminar, possibly accompanied by a PowerPoint presentation with far too many bullet points. But stick with me here because understanding this concept could be the superhero cape your business needs to shield you from the slings and arrows of outrageous fortune —or at least from the potential financial pitfalls of business ownership.

At its core, limited liability is the legal principle that protects your personal assets (like your home, car, and grandma's heirloom necklace) from being seized to cover business debts and liabilities. If your LLC faces a lawsuit or defaults on its debts, your personal assets are typically off-limits. This protection hinges on the LLC being a separate legal entity distinct from its owners. It's akin to imagining your business as a person with responsibilities and a bank account. You wouldn't want to be personally liable for your neighbor's debts. Well, in the eyes of the law, your LLC and you are just neighbors.

This separation provides a comforting layer of security for business owners who might otherwise be exposed to significant risks. For example, consider a contractor who renovates homes. In the unfortunate event of a structural issue that leads to a lawsuit, the contractor's personal assets could be targeted without an LLC. Only the business's assets would typically be at risk with an LLC.

However, like all superheroes, the power of limited liability isn't without its kryptonite. There are certain situations where this veil of protection can be pierced. For instance, if you personally guarantee a loan for your LLC and the business fails to meet its repayment obligations, you could still be on the hook. Similarly, if there's evidence of fraudulent behavior or if you combine personal and business funds (a big no-no!), you might find that the legal shield of your LLC won't hold up in court.

Let's look at a real-life scenario to illustrate these points better. Consider the case of a small boutique shop, Chic Fashions LLC, owned by Maria. She diligently used her business account to manage all shop-related transactions. However, during a particularly tight month, she paid her suppliers from her personal account. This act of commingling funds could jeopardize her limited liability protection by blurring the lines between personal and business finances.

It's a simple mistake but one that could have significant legal implications.

Moreover, while the concept of limited liability sounds bulletproof, it's not a magical force field that always protects you. It requires you to maintain the legal integrity of your LLC by following all necessary formalities and keeping thorough documentation. This means regular filing of the required paperwork, keeping personal and business finances distinctly separate, and understanding where your responsibilities as an owner begin and end.

Understanding these nuances is crucial for your peace of mind and your business's sustained health and legal standing. It's about knowing the rules of the game and playing it smart, ensuring that while you strive for success, you are also building a fortress around the personal life you've worked so hard to create. This blend of ambition and prudence is what marks a savvy entrepreneur. So, while "limited liability" might not be the most exhilarating phrase, its implications are profound, acting as a sentinel guarding the gateway between your business endeavors and personal life.

1.3 UNDERSTANDING THE DIFFERENT TYPES OF LLCS

If you've ever found yourself at a bustling artisan coffee shop, you might have noticed that no two lattes are the same. Some prefer them sweet, others bold, and a few might choose something unique, like a lavender-infused espresso. Much like crafting the perfect cup of coffee, selecting the correct type of LLC for your business can be a nuanced affair tailored to meet specific needs and preferences. Let's navigate through the different LLC types, similar to selecting your ideal coffee blend, ensuring you know your options and can pick what best suits your business recipe.

Single-Member vs. Multi-Member LLCs

The most straightforward distinction in LLCs is between single-member and multi-member formats, akin to deciding whether to have a quiet coffee alone or invite friends to join you. A single-member LLC is precisely what it sounds like— one owner fully controls the business. This setup is perfect for solo entrepreneurs who are looking to keep their business operations straightforward while still enjoying the liability protection and tax benefits of an LLC. It's concise, with fewer management and profit distribution formalities— everything flows directly to the sole member.

On the other hand, a multi-member LLC is like a coffee club —ownership is shared. This structure allows multiple members to own a portion of the business, which is ideal for partnerships or groups looking to pool resources and share the business's responsibilities. However, with more members involved, it's crucial to have a well-drafted operating agreement outlining each member's investment, responsibilities, profit share, and what happens if someone decides to leave the coffee club. The complexity of managing a multi-member LLC increases as decisions need to be made collectively, and profits are distributed according to the agreed-upon percentages in the operating agreement.

Professional LLCs (PLLCs)

Transitioning from the general to the specific, let's talk about professional LLCs, or PLLCs. This variant is tailor-made for professionals who require state licenses to offer their services—think doctors, lawyers, architects, and accountants. States that allow PLLCs often require that all members of the LLC be licensed professionals in the field in which the LLC operates. This not only reinforces credibility but also provides a structured way for professionals to benefit from the liability protection and tax treatments of an LLC while meeting the regulatory standards of their profession.

The benefits of forming a PLLC are significant, especially in protecting personal assets from claims related to business debts. However, it's important to note that individual liability for professional malpractice remains on the table. For instance, if a physician in a PLLC is sued for malpractice, the liability protection of an LLC won't shield their personal assets from that particular claim. However, it does protect against unrelated business debts. This nuanced protection makes PLLCs a strategic choice for professionals looking to balance the operational flexibility of an LLC with the demands of professional regulation.

Series LLCs

Imagine you have a coffee shop that also sells bakery items and hosts live music events. A series LLC can be likened to managing these ventures under one big umbrella while keeping their finances and liabilities distinct, like having separate tabs for each service in the shop. This type of LLC is particularly intriguing for entrepreneurs who run multiple related business ventures. It allows them to categorize assets and liabilities in separate series or cells under the central LLC umbrella, thereby isolating the risks of one venture from affecting the others.

However, not all states recognize series LLCs, which require careful adherence to operational separation between each series. This means maintaining distinct records and bank accounts for each series and delineating assets and liabilities. The appeal lies in the efficiency of setting up a new series under the primary LLC without the costs and paperwork of forming an entirely new entity, much like adding a new coffee blend to the menu without opening a new shop.

L3Cs

Lastly, let's delve into L3Cs, a special breed of LLC designed for ventures that prioritize social objectives over profits. These "low-profit limited liability companies" blend the financial advantages of LLCs with the social benefits of a nonprofit organization. They're structured to attract private and philanthropic investments, ideally suited for businesses with a charitable or educational mission at their core but still operate in a commercial capacity.

An L3C is crafted to qualify as a suitable investment for certain foundations looking to fulfill their philanthropic goals through program-related investments (PRIs). By providing clear, mission-oriented goals that align with charitable purposes, L3Cs can tap into a unique funding pool, combining the flexibility and protection of an LLC with access to capital that typically flows into more traditional nonprofit channels. It's a compelling model for socially conscious entrepreneurs who are looking to brew a business that not only serves coffee but also serves the community.

1.4 COMPARING LLCS WITH OTHER BUSINESS STRUCTURES: WHICH ONE FITS BEST?

When deciding on the structure of your new business, it's like choosing between different types of vehicles. Each model offers distinct features and must be determined based on terrain, budget, and the journey ahead. Similarly, selecting a business structure isn't just about preference; it's about what fits the nature of your business, the level of liability you're comfortable with, and how you plan to handle your taxes. So, let's take a detailed look at how an LLC compares to other business structures like sole proprietorships, corporations, and partnerships.

LLC vs. Sole Proprietorship

Starting with the simplest structure, a sole proprietorship is like a bicycle. It's straightforward, easy to manage, and doesn't require much paperwork. However, like riding a bike on a busy highway, operating as a sole proprietor can expose you to risks. There's no legal distinction between you and your business. If your business incurs debt or faces legal action, your assets could be at risk. In contrast, an LLC provides that crucial separation between your personal assets and business liabilities—like upgrading to an armored vehicle. Additionally, while both structures benefit from pass-through taxation, the LLC can choose a different tax status if beneficial, providing flexibility as your business grows and evolves.

Taxation for sole proprietors is straightforward as it involves reporting your business income and expenses on your personal tax return. However, this simplicity also means missing out on some of the tax benefits an LLC can offer, such as potential savings on self-employment taxes or the option to be taxed as an S-corporation. Operational flexibility is another consideration. Sole proprietorships are easy to set up and manage, perfect for low-risk businesses or side projects. However, if you're looking at a company that might grow or where liability could be a concern, the LLC offers a structure that scales with your needs while keeping things relatively simple.

LLC vs. Corporation

Moving on to corporations, think of them as buses—capable of carrying more passengers but also being more complex to operate. Corporations, particularly C-corps, offer strong protection against liability, much like LLCs. The critical difference lies in their tax treatment and regulatory requirements. Corporations face double taxation—once at the corporate level and again on dividends paid to shareholders. This can be mitigated by electing an S-corp tax status, which, similar to an LLC, allows profits and losses to pass through to personal tax returns, avoiding double taxation.

However, corporations require a more rigid structure, including a board of directors, corporate officers, and regular shareholder meetings. This can be cumbersome for small businesses or solo entrepreneurs who prefer simplicity and flexibility. In this context, an LLC is like a private car—less bulky than a bus, suitable for fewer passengers, and easier to maneuver. Entrepreneurs often choose an LLC over a corporation to avoid extensive record-keeping, rigid structures, and double taxation while enjoying liability protection and tax options.

LLC vs. Partnership

Comparing an LLC to a partnership is like comparing a sports team to a doubles tennis match. Both are team efforts, but the scale and dynamics differ significantly. Partnerships, particularly general partnerships, are straightforward in formation and operation, much like sole proprietorships, with all partners actively managing the business. However, in a general partnership, each partner is personally liable for the debts and obligations of the company. This is a significant risk, mainly if you only partially control some decisions.

LLCs provide a similar collaborative opportunity for multiple owners but with the added shield of limited liability. This means that, unlike in a partnership, your assets are generally protected from business liabilities. Additionally, while partnerships benefit from pass-through taxation, LLCs offer more flexibility in how profits and losses are distributed among members, which can be tailored in the operating agreement and don't necessarily have to match the ownership percentages.

Decision-Making Guidance

Choosing the proper business structure is crucial and should be based on specific factors, including the potential risks associated with your business, financial goals, and growth aspirations. An LLC is often the preferred choice for those looking to retain personal liability protection while enjoying flexibility in management and tax options. It provides a balanced mix of security, flexibility, and simplicity, ideal for many small to medium-sized businesses and startups. However, a corporation might be the right fit for businesses that anticipate raising significant outside capital or going public due to its familiar structure and ability to issue stock.

Assess your business needs, consult a financial advisor or a legal expert, and consider how each structure aligns with your long-term business goals and personal risk tolerance. This decision is foundational to your business's success and your peace of mind as an entrepreneur.

1.5 THE ROLE OF ARTICLES OF ORGANIZATION IN YOUR LLC

Imagine you're setting up a new smartphone for the first time. You're prompted to enter crucial information to get everything up and running: your name, password, and perhaps fingerprint. Without these, the phone is just a shiny gadget, but with them, it springs to life, tailored to your needs. Similarly, the Articles of Organization are foundational when forming your LLC. They aren't just paperwork; they bring your business entity to life in the eyes of the law.

The Articles of Organization, sometimes called the Certificate of Formation or Certificate of Organization, depending on your state, are the birth certificates for your LLC. They officially register your business with the state and are crucial for legally establishing your LLC's existence. If you file this document, your business legally exists, and you can enjoy all of the protections and benefits an LLC offers. It's the step that separates your business activities from personal endeavors, ensuring that your personal assets are shielded from business liabilities. This document is your LLC's official claim to its name, signifying to the world, and more importantly to the legal system, that your business is an entity in its own right, capable of owning property, entering into contracts, and suing or being sued.

Filing the Articles of Organization is straightforward but varies slightly from state to state. Generally, you'll file with the Secretary of State's office or a similar agency that handles business filings. Depending on your location, the filing fee varies, ranging from $50 to $500. You can often file online, or if you prefer paper, you can mail in your application. Here's a quick tip: Ensure all your information is correct before submitting it. A typo in your business name or address could lead to significant headaches, including needing to file amendments that might cost you additional fees.

Now, what goes into these Articles of Organization? While the specifics can vary by state, certain key components are almost universally required:

- **Name of the LLC:** This needs to comply with your state's naming requirements, which typically include making sure the name isn't already in use and consists of an indicator of its status as an LLC, like "LLC" or "Limited Company."
- **Principal place of business:** This is where your business's operations are based. It can be your home address if you are operating a home-based business.
- **Registered agent:** The registered agent is the person or service authorized to receive legal papers on behalf of your LLC. This role is crucial as they are your point of contact for legal documents, including potential lawsuits and tax notices.
- **Duration of the LLC:** While most LLCs are set up to continue indefinitely, some states require you to specify if there's a planned end date.
- **Purpose of the LLC:** Some states require you to describe the purpose of your business, though often a general statement like "to conduct any lawful business" is sufficient.

As your business grows and evolves, your initial filings might need updates. Changes in your business, like a new address, a change in registered agents, or even a change in the business purpose, require you to file an amendment to your Articles of Organization. Staying current is not just about compliance; it's about ensuring that the legal protections of your LLC remain intact. Most states have a simple process for filing amendments, which can often be completed online for a fee.

Filing your Articles of Organization is like setting the foundation for your house. Getting it right is crucial, as everything else will build upon this initial step. With the correct setup, you ensure your LLC is recognized legally, paving the way for everything from opening business bank accounts to entering into contracts while protecting your personal assets. Though wrapped in bureaucratic nuances, this foundational step empowers you to build your business on solid ground, ensuring it's equipped to handle whatever challenges and opportunities lie ahead.

THE INITIAL STEPS TO FORMING YOUR LLC

Imagine you've decided to throw the most epic dinner party. You've got visions of a feast that will be talked about for years, a true pièce de résistance. But before you even think about what's on the menu, there's one thing you need to nail down: the name of the soirée. It must be catchy, memorable, and—above all—give your guests a taste of the splendid evening ahead. Just as the name of your dinner party sets the tone for a delightful evening, the name of your LLC sets the stage for your business's identity and its journey in the marketplace. It's not just a label; it's the first whisper of all your business promises.

2.1 CHOOSING A COMPLIANT AND CATCHY NAME FOR YOUR LLC

Importance of a Unique Name

The name of your LLC is more than just a moniker—it's its identity, first impression, and brand all rolled into one. Choosing the right name is crucial; it must resonate with your target audience, reflect your company's ethos, and be unique. A distinctive name helps avoid confusion in the market, ensuring your business stands out in a sea of competitors. More critically, it avoids legal snafus that could arise from trademark infringement if your chosen name treads too close to that of another entity. The last thing you want is a legal battle over a name before launching your first product or service.

State-Specific Naming Rules

Each state in the U.S. has its own set of rules regarding business names. Generally, your LLC's name must include an indicator of its entity type, such as "LLC," "L.L.C.," or "Limited Liability Company," to clarify that it's an LLC and not some other type of business structure. Moreover, there are usually restrictions on using certain words like "Bank," "University," or "Hospital" unless you have the specific licenses to operate as one. These rules are not just bureaucratic red tape; they prevent misleading the public about what your business does.

Search for Availability

So, you've brainstormed a list of potential names, each more brilliant than the last. Before you get too attached, you must make sure the name you love is available for use. This involves a bit of detective work. You'll need to conduct a name search through your state's business filings—often available on the Secretary of State's website—to see if your chosen name is already in use. Think of it as a treasure hunt, where the treasure is a name that not only ticks all your boxes but is also free and clear for you to claim as your own.

Tips for a Catchy Name

Your LLC's name should be a beacon, drawing in customers and making a memorable impression. Here are a few tips to craft a name that sticks:

- **Please keep it simple and pronounceable:** A tongue-twister name might be memorable for the wrong reasons.
- **Be descriptive but not too literal:** Give your customers a hint of what you do without boxing yourself in. "Springfield Digital Marketing Solutions" is descriptive, but "Springfield Digital Dynamo" might have more spark while leaving room for future growth.
- **Use rhythmic and alliterative qualities:** Names that rhyme or have a rhythm to them, like "Cocoa Bean Coffee Co." are pleasing to say and highly memorable.

- **Avoid narrow geographical names unless local is your focus:** Naming your business "Nevada Network Solutions" might be a drawback if you expand beyond Nevada.

Choosing the right name for your LLC is like setting up the first domino in a series; it will impact your brand, marketing, and business's core identity. Take your time, follow these guidelines, and choose a name that will resonate well with your target market and align with your long-term vision. Remember, this is the first step in translating your entrepreneurial vision into a tangible entity. Make it count.

2.2 NAVIGATING STATE-SPECIFIC LLC REGULATIONS EFFICIENTLY

When you decide to set up an LLC, it's like planning a road trip across the United States; each state you pass through might have different speed limits, road rules, and scenic stops. Similarly, each state has its own set of rules and regulations for forming and running an LLC. These variations can significantly affect everything from how you structure your business to how much you pay in taxes. Understanding and adhering to these state-specific laws is not just about compliance; it's about optimizing your business for success and sustainability in its home state.

The differences in state laws can be broad and deep. For example, some states require an LLC to have more than one member, while others allow single-member LLCs. Some states levy a state tax on LLCs; others do not. Then, annual reporting requirements can vary drastically in the information required and the frequency with which it must be submitted. In California, for instance, LLCs must pay an annual minimum franchise tax, which must be factored into their business budget. Meanwhile, in Wyoming, LLCs benefit from no state corporate or personal income taxes, which can be a tremendous saving and a big draw for business owners.

Critical regulatory considerations include understanding the minimum capital requirements to start an LLC in your state. While most states do not have a minimum capital requirement, some states, like Nevada, require specific information about your business's capitalization to be included in your Articles of Organization. Another significant area is the annual reporting obligations that help maintain your LLC's good standing with the state. These reports typically include updates on addresses, management, and registered agent information. Neglecting these can lead to fines or even the administrative dissolution of your LLC.

For reliable resources, state government websites are primary sources of up-to-date and accurate information regarding LLC regulations. Each state's Secretary of State website provides detailed information on the requirements for forming and maintaining an LLC, including necessary forms and fee schedules. Additionally, legal databases such as LexisNexis or Westlaw can offer more detailed insights and case law that can be helpful if you're navigating more complex legal issues related to your LLC.

Let's look at practical examples to illustrate how businesses successfully navigate these regulatory waters. Consider a tech startup that initially formed an LLC in Massachusetts, where the laws favored their business model, allowing flexible profit distributions. As the business grew, the owners decided to expand into Florida. They quickly realized that Florida required more frequent reporting and a different tax structure. By consulting with a legal advisor and using online resources from the Florida Division of Corporations, they could adjust their operations to meet Florida's specific requirements without disrupting their business. Another example is a consulting firm in Colorado that took advantage of the state's business-friendly tax laws, which do not require LLCs to pay state taxes on pass-through income. This provided significant savings, allowing the firm to invest more in expanding its services.

Understanding and adapting to state-specific LLC regulations is crucial for your business's compliance and success. It ensures that your LLC starts on the right legal footing and continues to operate efficiently and profitably in its chosen state. By staying informed and proactive about these regulations, you can steer your business clear of legal pitfalls and toward a path of sustained growth and success.

2.3 DESIGNATING A RELIABLE REGISTERED AGENT

Think of a registered agent as the reliable friend who always reminds you about your car's oil change, except, in this case, it's about handling potentially critical legal documents and maintaining smooth communication with the state on behalf of your LLC. This isn't just any administrative role—it's a pivotal function that keeps your business in good legal standing. The registered agent receives service of process notices, government correspondence, and compliance-related documents. If your business gets sued or the state needs to talk to your LLC, the registered agent is the first point of contact. This role is vital because missing out on these notices due to an unreliable agent can lead to serious legal repercussions, including the default judgment against your business if you fail to respond to a lawsuit in time.

When choosing a registered agent, the first criterion is reliability. This person or service must be impeccably reliable and always available during business hours to receive and process documents promptly. Think of it as choosing a babysitter for your child; you wouldn't pick someone who isn't dependable. Next, consider the location. Your registered agent must be physically located in the state where your LLC is registered, as they need to be available to receive service of process in person. This rule is strict; having an agent outside your LLC's state is not just impractical, it's against the rules.

Now, you may ask whether to appoint someone you know, a lawyer, or yourself or go with a professional service. Each option has its pros and cons. Appointing yourself or an acquaintance can be cost-effective and straightforward. Keeping things within your known circle where trust is established feels good. However, this can mix personal and professional life in ways that might only sometimes be ideal. There's also the matter of privacy. Remember, the registered agent's address is a public record, which means anyone can see it. If you're operating your business from home, are you comfortable with your home address being out there for the world to see?

Using a professional registered agent service, on the other hand, can provide privacy and a sense of security. These services are in the business of reliability and are equipped to handle legal documents properly and promptly. They can also help ensure compliance by reminding you of important filing deadlines. The downside? It's an additional expense; every penny counts if you're starting on a shoestring budget. Moreover, there's a less personal touch than someone you know and trust.

If you ever need to change your registered agent, the process, while straightforward, is crucial to get right. Each state has a form—usually titled "Change of Registered Agent" or something similar—that you need to fill out and file with the state agency that handles business filings. There's typically a small fee associated with this filing. The critical part here is timing and accuracy. Ensure the new agent is ready and capable of taking over without any coverage gap. Filing these changes correctly and promptly ensures that there's no period during which your LLC is without a registered agent, which could put your business at risk of missing essential notices.

Choosing the right registered agent is more than just ticking a box on your LLC setup checklist. It's about ensuring your business has the proper support structure to handle legal challenges efficiently and effectively. Whether you opt for a professional service or appoint a trusted acquaintance, make sure you understand the responsibilities and requirements of the role. After all, in the unpredictable seas of business, your registered agent is both your anchor and your lookout, keeping your business stable and informed. Choose wisely, and ensure they have what it takes to support your business's journey through its legal obligations.

2.4 DRAFTING YOUR LLC OPERATING AGREEMENT: A STEP-BY-STEP GUIDE

The operating agreement for your LLC is essentially the backbone of your business structure, much like a script for a well-coordinated play. It outlines who does what, the rules everyone plays by, and what happens if someone forgets their lines. This document is crucial for defining the internal workings of your LLC, laying out the rights and responsibilities of the members, and ensuring that everyone is on the same page—literally and figuratively. Even if you are the sole member of your LLC, having this document in place is akin to having a roadmap for your business's future. It clarifies your business structure to banks, creditors, and even legal situations, underscoring the professionalism and seriousness with which you approach your venture.

Purpose of an Operating Agreement

At its core, the operating agreement serves to codify the operations of your LLC, providing guidelines for its governance and the business relationships between its members. This agreement is essential because it overrides the default rules imposed by state laws without such a document. Without it, your LLC could be subject to generic state statutes that may not be suited to your business's unique needs. For example, some states distribute profits equally among members regardless of their initial investment unless an agreement specifies otherwise. So, if you and a partner have different investment stakes and contributions, an operating agreement allows you to outline profit shares that reflect your arrangement rather than mindlessly splitting it 50/50.

Key Components to Include

Your LLC's operating agreement should be as unique as your business, but several key components should be included to ensure comprehensiveness and clarity:

- **Member Roles and Responsibilities:** Clearly define who the members are, their contributions to the LLC, and their roles within the company. Are members expected to contribute a certain amount of capital, or are there expectations regarding providing services or expertise?
- **Voting Rights and Procedures:** Outline how decisions are made within the LLC. What issues require a vote, and what percentage is needed for a decision to pass? This section should detail the process for ordinary and significant decisions like amending the operating agreement or dissolving the LLC.
- **Profit Distribution:** Profits and losses can be a source of contention in any business. Your operating agreement should clearly state how members will be divided. Are they distributed according to ownership percentages, or is another arrangement in place?
- **Management Structure:** Will your LLC be member-managed or manager-managed? In a member-managed setup, all members share in the decision-making responsibilities. In a manager-managed setup, a designated member-manager or an outside

manager takes on the decision-making roles, possibly in exchange for a salary or a different profit share.

Customizing to Fit Specific Needs

Unlike corporate bylaws, which tend to follow a more standardized format, the beauty of an operating agreement lies in its flexibility, which allows you to tailor the provisions to fit the specific needs of your LLC. For instance, if your LLC is family-owned and operated, you might include provisions for the succession of membership, detailing how members' shares will be handled in the event of a member's death or incapacity. If your LLC has a specific mission or ethical stance, you might include clauses that ensure business practices align with these values.

Legal Validation

While crafting your operation on your own might seem economical, it's wise to have it reviewed by a legal professional. This isn't just about dotting your i's and crossing your t's; it's about ensuring that your agreement complies with state laws and protects your interests in various scenarios. A legal expert can provide insights that prevent ambiguous language and close loopholes, which could otherwise lead to disputes or legal challenges down the line. They can ensure that your operating agreement is airtight, with clear, enforceable terms in a court of law.

Creating a robust operating agreement is like setting the stage for a successful play. It requires thoughtful consideration, detailed scripting, and an understanding of the roles everyone plays. With a solid agreement, your LLC is better equipped to navigate the complexities of business operations, providing a transparent governance and conflict resolution framework. This document isn't just a formality—it's the playbook for your business's success, ensuring that every member knows the rules of the game and how to play their part effectively.

2.5 ESSENTIAL DOCUMENTS AND FILINGS FOR STARTING YOUR LLC

Starting your LLC feels a bit like setting up a new smartphone—you need to get through some initial setups and installations before you can enjoy the full functionality. The same goes for your LLC; there are some essential documents and filings that need to be handled to ensure your business starts on the right foot legally and financially. Let's break down these initial steps to ensure your LLC setup is as smooth as a well-oiled machine.

First, filing the Articles of Organization with your state is like pressing the power button on that new smartphone. This document is the official start of your LLC's legal life; without it, you're just a collection of ideas. The filing process involves submitting a document that includes essential information about your LLC, such as its name, principal office address, and contact information for its registered agent. Each state has its form and filing requirements, and typically, there's a fee involved—ranging from as little as $50 to as much as $500. While it might be tempting to breeze through these forms, take your time. Ensure every detail is accurate to prevent issues down the line. Many states offer online filing, which can speed up the approval process and get your LLC up and running faster.

Once your LLC is officially formed, your next step is to obtain an Employer Identification Number (EIN) from the IRS. Think of the EIN as your LLC's Social Security number. The IRS assigns a unique nine-digit number to your business entity for tax purposes. You'll need this not just for filing taxes but also for opening a bank account in the name of your LLC and handling employee payroll, should you have employees. The good news? It's free and can be obtained quickly through the IRS's online application system. Once submitted, you typically receive your EIN immediately, allowing you to move forward with other setups without delay.

Moving forward, depending on the nature of your business and its location, you might need specific permits and licenses to operate legally. This part can get tricky, as requirements vary significantly by state, municipality, and industry. For instance, if you're opening a restaurant, you'll need health permits, liquor licenses, and possibly even a music license. These are not just bureaucratic checkboxes. They are essential for ensuring that your business operates within the legal frameworks set by local, state, and federal agencies. Failing to obtain the necessary permits can lead to fines, shutdowns, or worse. To navigate this, utilize resources such as your local Chamber of Commerce or the Small Business Administration (SBA), which can guide what specific licenses and permits your LLC will need.

Finally, let's talk about record-keeping. From the moment your LLC is formed, keeping meticulous records is not just good practice—it's a legal safeguard. This includes everything from your initial Articles of Organization to membership agreements, operating agreements, financial statements, and records of all licenses and permits. Proper record-keeping supports your business's compliance with state and federal laws and comes in handy during tax season or if your LLC faces legal scrutiny. It's like keeping a detailed diary of your business's life; every entry, from a minor membership update to a significant financial transaction, should be accurately recorded and safely stored.

All these steps—from filing the Articles of Organization to meticulous record-keeping—lay the foundational stones of your LLC. They don't just fulfill legal requirements; they protect your business's interests and pave the way for its long-term success. By handling these early steps thoroughly, you ensure your LLC is built on a solid, compliant, and efficient base, ready to take on the business world.

As we close this chapter on the initial setups and filings for your LLC, remember that each step, each document, and each filing is a building block for your business. They are the initial brushstrokes on the canvas of your entrepreneurial masterpiece. In the next chapter, we'll dive into managing your LLC's finances, from setting up your accounting systems to understanding and maximizing your tax benefits. This financial groundwork is crucial for keeping your business healthy and primed for growth. So, let's keep the momentum going, ensuring your LLC starts strong and continues to thrive.

FINANCIAL FOUNDATIONS FOR YOUR LLC

In the grand theater of entrepreneurship, setting up the financial infrastructure for your LLC is akin to laying down the electrical grid before opening night. It's not the most glamorous part of the show, but without it, nothing lights up. Your LLC's financial framework ensures that every transaction illuminates your business path, rather than casting it into darkness. So, let's turn the spotlights on one of the first and most critical steps: establishing your LLC's bank account. Think of it as setting up the box office where all your earnings will be securely managed and accounted for.

3.1 SETTING UP YOUR LLC BANK ACCOUNT: A FOOLPROOF PROCESS

Importance of a Dedicated Business Account

Why is having a dedicated bank account for your LLC as crucial as having a script for an actor? First, it draws a clear, legal line between your personal and business finances. This separation is essential for keeping your financial records straight and protecting your personal assets. If your company faces legal scrutiny, a clearly defined boundary between your personal and business finances helps maintain the liability protection that an LLC structure offers. It's like having a fire door between your living room and a burning kitchen—keeping the flames contained.

Furthermore, a dedicated business account simplifies every aspect of your financial management, from accounting to tax reporting. It allows you to track business expenses accurately, manage cash flow, and prepare financial statements that reflect the proper financial health of your business. Imagine trying to perform heart surgery with mixed-up surgical tools; similarly, mixed finances can lead to messy complications that might hinder the growth and scalability of your business.

Choosing the Right Bank and Account Type

Selecting where to park your business funds is more complex than picking the nearest bank or sticking with where you have a personal account. This decision warrants a thoughtful comparison, much like choosing the right stage for your play. Consider fees, services offered, location convenience, and online banking services. Each bank offers different perks and packages for business accounts. Some offer free transactions up to a specific limit, others provide better interest rates, and some excel in customer service.

Deciding between a checking, savings, or credit account is also crucial. A checking account is essential for day-to-day transactions, paying bills, and handling business expenses. Consider a savings account to set aside a portion of your business income for future investment or as a reserve for slower business periods. A credit account can be helpful for businesses that need to purchase inventory or equipment. Still, managing this wisely is crucial to avoid accumulating debt that could stifle your business growth.

Documentation Required for Account Setup

Roll up your sleeves to set up your LLC bank account—it's paperwork time. You'll need your LLC's EIN (Employer Identification Number), which acts like your business's Social Security number. This is a must-have for tax purposes and to legally identify your business. You'll also need copies of your Articles of Organization, which verify your LLC's legal registration and existence. Lastly, bring your operating agreement, if you have one, as it outlines your LLC's owner-ship structure, operating procedures, and information that banks might require to open your account.

Managing Your Account

Once your account is up and running, managing it effectively is vital to maintaining the financial integrity of your LLC. Implement online banking to monitor your account actively, ensuring you're always aware of your financial status. Consider setting up multiple signatories if your LLC has more than one member; this not only aids in transparency but also ensures that all economic activities are overseen by more than one person, adding an extra layer of security.

Regular reviews of your account will help you stay on top of your finances, catch discrepancies early, and make informed decisions based on your financial standing. These reviews are like rehearsals before the performance, ensuring everything runs smoothly during showtime.

Establishing and managing your LLC's bank account might seem like a backstage task, but it's as crucial as the performance itself. It sets the stage for financial success, providing the security and structure needed to manage your business's finances effectively. As you continue to build your LLC, remember that this foundational step is just the beginning. Each transaction, big or small, is a brushstroke in the bigger picture of your business masterpiece.

3.2 BASIC BOOKKEEPING FOR LLCS: KEEPING YOUR FINANCES IN CHECK

Imagine stepping into a garden where every plant represents a different aspect of your business finances. Some plants symbolize your sales, others your expenses, and some even your investments in the business. Bookkeeping is the art of tending to this garden, ensuring every plant is healthy, accounted for, and adequately nurtured. It's not just about recording what grows and what withers; it's about understanding the ecosystem of your business's finances. Accurate bookkeeping does more than keep your financial garden thriving; it provides crucial data that helps you make informed decisions, ensures compliance with tax laws, and prepares you for financial audits.

The cornerstone of good bookkeeping starts with setting up a tailored bookkeeping system. In today's digital age, you have many options, ranging from traditional manual systems to sophisticated cloud-based solutions. Manual bookkeeping is akin to using hand tools in your garden—it's labor-intensive and time-consuming but can work for a very small or newly sprouted business. This system involves physical ledgers or simple spreadsheet software for manually making entries. It's cost-effective but prone to human error and can become overwhelming as your business grows.

On the other end of the spectrum are software-based and cloud-based systems, which are like upgrading to power tools. Software-based systems require installation on your computer and provide robust features that automate many bookkeeping tasks, such as generating invoices and financial statements. Cloud-based systems offer the same functionalities but with the added advantages of online access, integration with other digital tools, and real-time updates. These systems reduce the likelihood of errors and save time, allowing you to focus more on nurturing your business rather than maintaining its books.

Choosing the right system depends on your business size, financial complexity, and personal preference. For many modern businesses, cloud-based bookkeeping solutions are becoming the norm due to their efficiency and scalability. They allow you and your accountant to access financial data securely from anywhere, ensuring that your financial garden is tended to regularly and precisely.

Once your system is in place, the next crucial step is recording transactions accurately. Every business transaction must be recorded systematically, from the payment for a new office chair to the income from a big client project. Each entry should include the date, a clear description, the amount, and categorization (e.g., revenue, expense, capital contribution). This meticulous recording acts as the groundwork for all financial analysis and ensures that you can track the growth and health of your financial garden over time.

Regular reconciliation of your bookkeeping records with your bank statements is another vital practice, like regular weeding and pest control in your garden. This process involves matching the transactions in your bookkeeping records to those in your bank statement to ensure they align. Discrepancies might indicate errors or unauthorized transactions, and addressing these promptly helps maintain the health of your business finances. Regular reconciliations prepare you for smoother tax preparations and financial audits, as your records are consistently checked and kept in order.

Finally, preparing regular financial statements—the overview of your financial garden's health—is crucial. The two primary statements you'll focus on are the balance sheet and the profit and loss statement. The balance sheet provides a snapshot of your business's financial standing at a specific point in time, showing assets, liabilities, and equity. It's like taking a step back and assessing the health and growth of every plant in your garden. The profit and loss statement, or income statement, shows how much money the business made and spent. This document is essential for understanding the operational efficiency of your business, much like understanding which plants are thriving and which are not.

By embracing these bookkeeping practices, you ensure your financial garden is well-maintained and primed for growth. Accurate bookkeeping gives you the insights to make strategic decisions, like pruning back certain expenses to foster more robust growth in sales. It's not just about keeping the numbers; it's about understanding their story about your business's past and potential future. With each transaction recorded, reconciled, and reported, you're not just keeping books but writing the ongoing story of your business's financial journey.

3.3 BUDGETING STRATEGIES FOR EMERGING LLCS

Let's talk about budgeting—it's not just a spreadsheet filled with numbers and forecasts; it's the financial compass of your LLC. Think of budgeting as planning a road trip across the country. Without a map and a plan for how much you'll spend on gas, food, and lodging, you'd likely end up stranded or overspending. Similarly, a well-crafted budget guides your LLC by forecasting financial needs and maintaining discipline in spending, ensuring you don't find your business in a monetary pickle.

The beauty of a budget in the business world, especially for an LLC just finding its feet, is that it gives you control over your finances. It enables you to prioritize expenditures, track performance, and prepare for future financial needs. It's like having an economic blueprint that shows where you're allocating resources and where you can afford to dream bigger. For instance, if you're eyeing that sleek new office space or the latest tech to boost your productivity, your budget tells you when and if you can afford to make those leaps. More importantly, it helps prevent overspending, ensuring you're not dipping into funds allocated for crucial expenses like rent or vendor payments.

Creating a startup budget might seem daunting, but it's about understanding your business's operational flow during its initial phase. Start by listing all possible expenses—one-time costs like purchasing equipment and ongoing costs such as utility bills and salaries. Don't forget to include a buffer for unexpected expenses; the business world is often unpredictable, and having a financial cushion can save you from many headaches. Next, project your revenue. This can be challenging, especially if you don't have historical data to rely on, but be conservative in your estimates. Overestimating revenue can lead to financial decisions that might stretch your LLC's finances too thin.

Projecting revenue involves understanding your market and your business's capacity. For instance, if you're opening a local coffee shop, look at factors like foot traffic, average sales in the area, and seasonal fluctuations in business. This part of budgeting is much like forecasting weather for a sailing trip—you need to know when to expect smooth sailing and when to prepare for potential storms.

Monitoring and adjusting your budget are where the real magic happens. This ongoing process allows you to compare your projected figures with actual performance and make necessary adjustments. It's akin to tweaking your ingredients as you cook, ensuring the end product is just right. Regularly review your financial statements and check them against your budget. Are you spending more on supplies than anticipated? Is the revenue not meeting your projections? Understanding these variances will help you make informed decisions, like renegotiating vendor contracts or ramping up marketing efforts to boost sales.

In today's digital age, several tools and resources can simplify budgeting. Budgeting software or templates can automate calculations, track performance against budgets, and forecast future financial scenarios. These tools often come with dashboards that provide visual insights into your finances, making it easier to grasp where your money is going and where you might need to cut back or can afford to expand.

Investing time in creating and managing a budget might seem like a chore, especially when there are a hundred other tasks vying for your attention in the bustling early days of your LLC. However, this financial roadmap is crucial. It clarifies, controls spending, and prepares you for future financial needs, ensuring that your LLC can navigate the unpredictable waters of business with confidence and financial savvy. Like any great adventure, the success of your business journey largely depends on how well you plan your route and manage your resources along the way.

3.4 UNDERSTANDING PASS-THROUGH TAXATION AND ITS BENEFITS

Imagine if every dollar your LLC earned was taxed twice—once when it hit your business account and again when it landed in your personal pocket. Sounds pretty discouraging, right? Thankfully, there's something called pass-through taxation, a system that feels a bit like having a VIP pass at a concert. It lets profits from your LLC bypass the entity itself and get taxed just once at the owners' or members' personal income level. This mechanism is a fundamental attribute of most LLCs and is pivotal in understanding why this business structure can be so attractive.

Pass-through taxation means the LLC isn't taxed directly under federal income tax laws. Instead, the profits and losses of the business "pass through" to your personal tax return. This method contrasts sharply with traditional corporations (C-corps), where earnings are first taxed at the corporate level. Then, any dividends paid out to shareholders are taxed again on their personal tax returns. This dual hit can significantly whittle down what you take home. For an LLC, avoiding this scenario means more of the profits made from your sweat and tears end up in your pocket rather than being lost to layers of taxation.

This structure can translate into tangible tax savings for you, the LLC member. Depending on your personal income tax bracket, these savings can be substantial compared to other business structures. Additionally, this setup simplifies your tax filing process. You're not dealing with corporate tax returns; everything is consolidated into your personal return. This simplicity can be quite a relief, especially when you're wearing multiple hats in your business, and every minute saved is a minute you can spend growing your enterprise or catching your breath.

However, there's a twist in the tale regarding self-employment taxes. As an LLC member, the IRS considers you self-employed, which means you're responsible for covering Social

Security and Medicare taxes, commonly referred to as self-employment tax. These taxes are based on the total net earnings of the business, which is a different ball game compared to being an employee, where you share these tax responsibilities with your employer. Preparing for this can seem daunting, but think of it as investing in your future security. Regularly setting aside money from your business income to cover these taxes is crucial to managing this. It prevents year-end surprises and ensures you meet your tax obligations without a hitch.

Navigating the tax landscape can also vary significantly depending on where you've planted your business flag. While federal tax laws regarding LLCs are generally uniform, state-specific considerations can vary. Some states have additional taxes that could apply to your LLC earnings, or they might not recognize pass-through status and require state-level tax filing. Understanding these nuances is crucial. For instance, LLCs are subject to an annual franchise tax in California, a cost you must factor into your financial planning. Conversely, states like Wyoming offer a more tax-friendly environment with no state income tax, which can be a boon for your business's bottom line.

Incorporating knowledge about these state-specific quirks into your financial strategy is more than just compliance—it's about optimizing your business's potential. Each state's tax landscape can affect your decision-making, from how much you reinvest in business growth to strategic decisions about expanding into new territories. It's akin to understanding the climate of a region before deciding to plant a garden there. The better you know the conditions, the better you can plan for strong and sustainable growth.

Navigating the pass-through taxation system effectively requires a keen understanding and a proactive approach. It's about making the tax system work for you, maximizing your benefits while ensuring compliance. As you continue to steer your LLC through the complexities of the business world, keep these insights in mind. They help safeguard your earnings and empower you to make smarter decisions that bolster your business's financial health over the long haul.

3.5 TAX OBLIGATIONS FOR LLCS: WHAT YOU NEED TO KNOW

Navigating the tax landscape as an LLC owner is like planning a large-scale event; there are many moving parts, and missing even a small detail can lead to significant headaches. Understanding your tax obligations is crucial not only for compliance but also for optimizing your financial strategy. Let's peel back the layers of federal and state tax obligations to ensure you're compliant and possibly saving money.

Federal Tax Responsibilities

At the federal level, your LLC is treated as a pass-through entity, meaning income earned flows through to the owners' or members' personal tax returns. However, it's about more than just reporting income; there are several other tax responsibilities you need to be aware of. First, if your LLC has employees, you're responsible for withholding payroll taxes. This includes withholding income tax and the employee's portion of Social Security and Medicare taxes. Additionally, as an employer, you must pay the employer's portion of

Social and Medicare taxes, which equates to matching the amounts withheld from your employees.

Another critical aspect is the payment of estimated taxes. Since income from your LLC isn't subject to withholding, you (and any other members) will likely need to make quarterly estimated tax payments if you expect to owe $1,000 or more when your return is filed. These payments cover your income tax and self-employment tax liabilities. It's similar to pacing yourself in a marathon; rather than dealing with a daunting tax bill all at once, you spread it out to manage your cash flow better and avoid underpayment penalties.

Lastly, it's essential to understand the forms involved. Form 1040 for your personal taxes is where you'll report LLC income, but there are additional forms depending on your situation. If you have employees, you'll need to file forms related to employment taxes, like Form 941, the employer's quarterly federal tax return. These forms ensure you correctly report the withholding and payment of employment taxes throughout the year.

State and Local Taxes

Just when you think you've got a handle on federal taxes, state and local taxes come into play, each with its own set of rules and rates. Most states require you to pay state income tax on your LLC's earnings, but how they assess and collect these taxes can vary dramatically. Some states, like Texas and Florida, do not have a state income tax, which can significantly impact your financial planning. Others, like New York and California, have state income taxes and additional taxes like franchise or gross receipts taxes that could apply to your LLC.

Apart from income taxes, you should be aware of sales tax obligations if your LLC sells goods or provides taxable services. If applicable, you'll need to collect sales tax from customers and remit it to the state. Each state has different rules about what types of goods and services are taxable, and rates can vary from state to state and between localities within a state.

Then, there are property taxes, which are assessed if your LLC owns real property. These taxes are based on the property's assessed value and are used to fund local projects and services like schools, roads, and public safety.

Tax Filing Requirements and Deadlines

Keeping track of tax filing requirements and deadlines is crucial to avoid penalties and interest charges for late filings or payments. The key dates generally include April 15 for annual returns, with quarterly estimated taxes typically due on April 15, June 15, September 15, and January 15 of the following year. However, specific filing deadlines can vary depending on state regulations, so confirming these dates with your local tax authority is essential.

Understanding the forms you need to file is just as important as when to file them. For instance, sales tax returns might need to be filed monthly, quarterly, or annually, depending on the amount of sales tax you collect, and each state has its own forms for income tax filings.

Seeking Professional Advice

Given the complexities and nuances of tax laws, consulting with a tax professional is not just recommended; it's a strategic move. A knowledgeable CPA or tax advisor can help ensure compliance with federal and state tax laws and offer strategies to minimize tax liabilities. They can be beneficial if your LLC operates in multiple states or has many employees, as these scenarios introduce additional complexity to your tax situation.

Engaging a tax professional can also provide peace of mind. Knowing an expert handles your taxes lets you focus more on running your business and less on deciphering tax codes. They can also keep you updated on changes in tax laws that might affect your LLC, ensuring you're always one step ahead.

Understanding and managing your tax obligations as an LLC owner is crucial for maintaining good legal standing and optimizing your financial outcomes. The spectrum of responsibilities can be daunting, from federal income and employment taxes to state-specific considerations like sales and property taxes. However, with careful planning, ongoing education, and the support of a skilled tax professional, you can navigate these waters successfully, keeping your LLC compliant and financially healthy.

As we wrap up this chapter on the financial foundations of your LLC, remember that each tax payment, each form filed, and each financial decision you make contributes to the broader narrative of your business. In the next chapter, we'll explore how to protect your assets and ensure your LLC's operations align with legal requirements and best practices, setting the stage for sustained success and growth.

LEGAL COMPLIANCE AND ASSET PROTECTION

Imagine you're a pirate navigating the treacherous waters of the Caribbean, not just for the thrill of adventure but to protect your precious cargo. Similarly, navigating the legal requirements of your LLC isn't just about adhering to rules —it's about safeguarding the treasure that is your business. In this chapter, we dive into the crucial, albeit somewhat less glamorous, world of compliance. It's not just about keeping your LLC on the right side of the law; it's about steering clear of the icebergs that could sink your entrepreneurial ship.

4.1 KEEPING YOUR LLC COMPLIANT WITH ANNUAL REQUIREMENTS

Understanding Annual Compliance

Just like a ship needs regular maintenance to stay seaworthy, your LLC must meet specific annual requirements to remain in good legal standing. Think of state authorities as the coast guards of business compliance; they ensure you navigate according to the rules, which typically include filing annual reports, paying franchise taxes, and renewing licenses and permits. These are not just bureaucratic hoops to jump through but vital processes that keep your business transparent and accountable, helping you maintain the trust of customers, investors, and the state.

Failing to comply with these annual rituals can be likened to ignoring a leak in your ship's hull. At first, it might not seem like a big deal, but over time, it can lead to severe problems that could have been easily avoided. The annual report, for example, updates the state of your LLC's activities and confirms your continued existence and operation. It's like sending a signal to the coast guards saying, "All's well!" Not sending this signal? Well, that might raise suspicions or concerns about your operational status.

Detailed Compliance Checklist

To keep your LLC shipshape, here's a detailed checklist to help you navigate the compliance waters:

1. **Annual Reports:** Check the due dates for your state. These reports typically include information on your LLC's current activities, addresses, and management structure.
2. **Franchise Taxes:** Not all states require them, but if yours does, know when and how much you need to pay. It's often calculated based on your LLC's earnings or the number of shares you hold.

3. **License and Permit Renewals:** You might need specific licenses and permits depending on your business type and location. Mark their expiration dates in your calendar to renew on time.

4. **Record Keeping:** Ensure all your LLC's operational records are up to date. This includes minutes of meetings, changes in membership or management, and financial transactions.

5. **Compliance with Local Laws:** Local county or city regulations sometimes have additional requirements. Keep a close eye on these to avoid local compliance issues.

Consequences of Noncompliance

Ignoring these requirements can lead to a cascade of legal and financial headaches. Penalty fees are just the start; more severe consequences can include losing good standing with the state and affecting your ability to secure funding or expand your business. In the worst-case scenario, your LLC could be administratively dissolved, leaving you without the liability protection that an LLC provides. It's like having your pirate ship impounded; suddenly, you're swimming with the sharks unprotected.

Resources for Compliance Assistance

Navigating these waters can be complex, especially if you're new to the world of entrepreneurship. Fortunately, you don't have to go it alone. Consider enlisting the help of compliance consultants or business legal services designed to keep your LLC in check. These services act like your navigational compass, keeping you on course through the murky waters of bureaucratic compliance. They can remind you of deadlines, help prepare the necessary documentation, and even file on your behalf, ensuring that your focus remains on steering your business to new horizons.

Remember, maintaining compliance isn't just about avoiding penalties; it's about ensuring your LLC can sail smoothly toward success, protected, and poised to capitalize on opportunities. Just as a well-maintained ship is more likely to withstand the challenges of the sea, a compliant LLC is equipped to navigate the complexities of the business world, making the most of its entrepreneurial voyage.

4.2 INSURANCE FOR LLCS: WHAT YOU NEED AND WHY

Imagine stepping out into a rainstorm without an umbrella —you can manage for a while, but soon, the discomfort becomes undeniable. Similarly, venturing into the business world without the right insurance is risky and potentially disastrous. Insurance for your LLC isn't just a safety net; it's essential gear that keeps the storm of unexpected liabilities from washing away your hard-earned success. Let's unpack the types of insurance that can shield your LLC and ensure that when storms hit, you're more than ready to weather them.

Types of Insurance for LLCs

Navigating the world of business insurance can feel like trying to find your way through a dense forest, with each type of insurance a different path offering unique forms of protection. **General liability insurance** is perhaps the most crucial—it's like the broad path that most travelers take. This insurance protects against claims of bodily injury or property damage that can occur during everyday business operations. Imagine a customer slipping on a wet floor in your office; general liability insurance helps cover medical costs and legal fees.

Then there's **professional liability insurance**, also known as errors and omissions (E&O) insurance, which is essential if your LLC provides professional services. This type of insurance covers you if a client claims that your services caused them financial harm due to mistakes or failure to perform. Think of it as the path through the woods fraught with roots and overhanging branches; professional liability insurance ensures you can navigate it without tripping.

Property insurance is crucial if your LLC owns physical assets like office space, equipment, or inventory. It covers damage to property from fire, theft, and, sometimes, natural disasters. Consider this the path through the forest that protects your physical assets from unexpected storms or falling trees.

Each type of insurance serves a unique purpose, addressing specific risks that can derail your LLC's journey. Understanding these types will help you choose the right coverage, ensuring you're adequately protected no matter your business's path.

Assessing Your Insurance Needs

Determining what insurance your LLC needs involves carefully evaluating your business activities, industry, and the risks associated with those operations. Start by considering the worst-case scenarios. What accidents or errors could potentially occur, and what would their impact be on your business? For instance, if you're in the construction industry, the risks of on-site injuries are high, making general liability and workers' compensation insurance indispensable.

Size also plays a role in assessing your needs. A small, home-based business might need a different level of coverage than a larger enterprise with multiple locations. But regardless of size, every company faces basic risks like property damage or legal liability, so starting with general liability insurance is wise.

Benefits of Adequate Insurance Coverage

The right insurance does more than comply with legal requirements—it provides peace of mind. With adequate coverage, you can focus on growing your LLC without worrying about potential lawsuits or disasters. Insurance protects not just your financial stability but also your reputation. It signals to clients, employees, and partners that you are responsible and prepared, which can be invaluable for building trust and credibility.

Moreover, certain types of insurance can be a gateway to opportunities. Some clients and projects require specific insurance before considering doing business with you. In this sense, having robust insurance coverage can open doors that might otherwise remain closed, facilitating growth and new ventures.

Shopping for Insurance

Choosing the right insurance provider is like choosing a guide for your hike through the woods—you need someone knowledgeable, reliable, and with the right resources. Start by comparing quotes from several insurance providers to understand what coverage options are available and at what cost. Don't just look at the price; consider the extent of coverage, the deductible amounts, and exclusions to ensure comprehensive protection.

Understanding policy terms is crucial. Insurance documents can be dense and filled with complex terminology, but take your time with this. Make sure to understand what each policy covers and what it doesn't. If necessary, consult with an insurance broker or a legal advisor who can help clarify the terms.

Lastly, don't be afraid to negotiate. Like many business services, there's often room to tailor terms to fit your needs better. Whether adjusting the coverage limits or negotiating the premiums, remember that your insurance policy is a critical part of your business strategy, and it should work for you, not against you.

Navigating the insurance landscape requires diligence, understanding, and a proactive approach. By thoroughly assessing your needs, understanding the benefits, and carefully selecting your provider, you ensure that your LLC is equipped to face the everyday risks and unexpected challenges that might arise. This level of preparedness is not just prudent; it's a strategic asset that fortifies your business, fostering growth, stability, and long-term success.

4.3 PROTECTING YOUR PERSONAL ASSETS FROM BUSINESS LIABILITIES

When you ventured into entrepreneurship, the thought of personal asset protection was a significant motivator for choosing the LLC structure. It's akin to installing a state-of-the-art security system in your home; it's there to protect your physical possessions and your peace of mind. However, maintaining this protective boundary requires more than a one-time setup; it demands ongoing vigilance and strategic fortification. Let's explore some crucial strategies to ensure that the liability shield of your LLC remains robust, guarding against any threats that might come its way.

One of the cornerstone practices for keeping your business veil intact is maintaining a crystal-clear separation between your personal and business finances. It might seem convenient to use your business account to pay for that new home espresso machine or vice versa, but blurring these lines can significantly weaken your LLC's liability protection. This financial intermingling can lead to what legal experts call "piercing the corporate veil," where courts can hold you personally liable for business debts because you treated your LLC's funds as your own. To fortify this boundary, always use separate bank accounts for personal and business transactions, and ensure all agreements, contracts, and receipts are clearly in the name of the LLC, not yours.

Moreover, adhering to all legal formalities can't be over-stressed. This means keeping up with all filings, resolutions, and records as diligently as a captain logs entries in a ship's ledger during a voyage. Regularly update your Articles of Organization and ensure your operating agreement reflects your LLC's current structure and operations. These documents are not just administrative necessities; they prove that your LLC functions as a separate legal entity, equipped to stand up to scrutiny should disputes arise.

Moving beyond basic practices, incorporating trusts and other legal structures can add layers of protection for your assets. Trusts, for example, can be a strategic choice for estate planning, ensuring that your assets are shielded from business liabilities and smoothly transitioned to your heirs. Assets in a properly structured trust are generally protected from personal and business creditors. This setup can be particularly advantageous if your business operations expose you to higher liability risks. Consulting with an estate planner or an attorney to tailor a trust to your specific needs can provide security and peace of mind, knowing that whatever the seas of business might toss your way, your personal assets will remain secure.

Another critical area to tread carefully is the realm of personal guarantees. New LLCs, especially those without a credit history, are often asked for personal guarantees on business loans or leases. While this can facilitate access to necessary funds or premises, it directly exposes your personal assets to risk. Before signing any agreement that involves a personal guarantee, consider the impacts carefully. Sometimes, negotiating better terms or providing alternative assurances, such as larger initial deposits or shorter lease terms, can mitigate the need for such guarantees. Always weigh the immediate benefits against the long-term risks. Remember, every signature you affix in the business world should be considered with the foresight of a chess master, anticipating moves several turns ahead.

Lastly, conducting regular legal audits can be your radar in the fog, helping identify potential vulnerabilities that could expose your personal assets. These audits can review everything from compliance with state laws to the adequacy of your insurance coverage. Should an audit reveal issues like outdated documentation, insufficient insurance, or compliance lapses, addressing these promptly can shore up your defenses, ensuring your LLC continues to provide the liability protection it was designed to offer.

Navigating these strategies effectively requires a blend of vigilance, foresight, and proactive management. By reinforcing your LLC's liability shield, exploring sophisticated asset protection strategies like trusts, being cautious with personal guarantees, and committing to regular legal audits, you not only protect your personal assets but also ensure the integrity and longevity of your business. Remember, the goal is not just to survive the entrepreneurial battles but to thrive amidst them, and having a solid defense strategy significantly tilts the odds in your favor.

4.4 INTELLECTUAL PROPERTY CONSIDERATIONS FOR LLCS

In the bustling marketplace of ideas and innovation that characterizes our modern economy, intellectual property (IP) is not just a legal asset but a cornerstone of competitive advantage. Imagine your LLC as a bustling café in the heart of a vibrant city; your unique recipes, the distinctive décor, and even the branded napkins are all forms of IP that set you apart from the café next door. For any LLC, recognizing and protecting intellectual property is akin to putting a lock on your café's door—it safeguards the elements that make your business unique and valuable. Let's explore how you can identify your IP assets and shield them effectively.

Identifying what constitutes intellectual property within your LLC might seem straightforward when considering patents or trademarks, but it extends further. It includes everything from your company logo and proprietary business processes to software code and even confidential data that gives you a market edge. Each of these assets is a vital ingredient in your business's success recipe and recognizing them is the first step in protection. For instance, if you've developed a unique software solution, it's not just the final product but also the source code, the user interface, and possibly the user experience elements that are your IP. Or, if you run a marketing firm, the research methods you've devised or even the advertising copy you create could be your intellectual property.

Once you've identified your IP, protecting it becomes your priority. This isn't just about locking away your secrets; it involves legal steps to ensure your intellectual assets are formally recognized and safeguarded. Registering your trademarks, for example, not only protects your brand identity but also ensures that you have exclusive rights to use it in your market sector within the geographical bounds where it's registered. Similarly, patents protect your inventions by giving you exclusive rights to make, use, or sell the invention for a certain period. Implementing confidentiality agreements with employees and partners is crucial even for nonregistrable IP, like trade secrets or proprietary processes. These agreements clarify that disclosing your business's secrets can have legal consequences, thus deterring misuse or unauthorized distribution.

Dealing with intellectual property infringement is something many LLCs may face as they grow. It's similar to someone trying to replicate your café's secret sauce without permission. The first step is ensuring a clear, enforceable IP policy. If infringement occurs, it generally starts with a cease-and-desist letter—a formal request to stop the infringing activity. If this isn't heeded, you may need to enforce your rights through litigation. Remember, acting swiftly is crucial to prevent further damage. However, ensuring you are not inadvertently infringing on others' IP rights is equally important. Regular IP audits, much like regular health checks, can help ensure your business respects existing IP rights and avoids costly legal battles.

Lastly, the strategic management of IP can significantly enhance your business's value and appeal. Strong, well-protected IP can be vital to attracting investors or potential buyers. They often see robust IP portfolios as a marker of a company's innovativeness and potential for sustained success. Moreover, IP can open new revenue streams through licensing or franchising, turning your intellectual assets into profitable ventures.

Navigating the complexities of intellectual property might seem daunting. Still, with the right strategies and protections, your LLC can defend its innovations and significantly leverage them for growth and success. Whether it's the secret recipe for your café's best-selling dish or a proprietary algorithm in your tech startup, understanding and protecting your intellectual property is critical to your business strategy.

4.5 NAVIGATING CONTRACTS AND LEGAL AGREEMENTS AS AN LLC

When running an LLC, entering into contracts isn't just a routine aspect of business—it's akin to setting the rules for how a game is played between your company and another party. Whether you're dealing with suppliers, customers, or partners, a well-drafted contract serves as your playbook, laying out the strategies, moves, and boundaries. It clarifies what's expected from each player, what's off-limits, and how conflicts on the field are handled, reducing misunderstandings and fostering a cooperative environment where each party understands their role and responsibilities.

The importance of these contracts can't be overstressed. They are fundamental in safeguarding your LLC's interests, mitigating risks, and setting clear expectations. A robust contract acts like a sturdy fence around your property; it keeps the good stuff in and the potential troubles out. It ensures everyone knows where they stand, which ultimately helps maintain healthy, professional relationships. For instance, a contract with a supplier might specify the quality of materials, delivery timelines, and payment terms, ensuring no surprises could disrupt your business operations.

Key Elements of Effective Contracts

Every contract your LLC enters into should be clear and comprehensive. Here are some key elements to ensure your contracts are solid and enforceable:

1. **Clear Terms and Conditions:** The heart of any contract is its terms and conditions. These should be as clear as possible, outlining what services or goods will be provided, pricing, and timelines. Ambiguity here can lead to disputes, so clarity is your best friend.

2. **Dispute Resolution Mechanisms:** It's optimistic to hope a business relationship will never run into turbulence, but it's wise to plan for such instances. Including a dispute resolution clause that outlines steps for handling disagreements, such as mediation or arbitration, can save both parties time and legal fees.

3. **Termination Clauses:** Sometimes, despite best efforts, relationships end. A termination clause outlines the conditions under which the contract can be ended by either party, the process for termination, and any responsibilities or penalties incurred upon termination.

4. **Confidentiality Agreements:** If your contract involves sharing sensitive information, a confidentiality clause is crucial to protect your business secrets and strategies.

5. **Liability Limits:** This clause limits the amount and types of damages one party can recover from the other. It's a way to manage risk and can be

particularly important in industries with a high potential for significant loss.

Negotiation Tactics

Negotiating a contract is much like a dance. It requires rhythm, respect, and a bit of give and take. When you negotiate, aim to create a win-win situation where both parties feel they are getting a fair deal. Keep your business objectives in mind, but also consider the relationship you want to maintain with the other party. Tactics like active listening, clear communication, and focused objectives can lead to successful negotiation outcomes. Always be prepared to walk away if the terms are unfavorable—knowing your nonnegotiables and limits is vital.

Handling Breaches and Disputes

Even with the best-drafted contracts, breaches can occur. When they do, refer back to your contract for the agreed-upon steps for resolution. If the breach is minor, reaching out to the other party and discussing ways to rectify the issue can often resolve the problem without further action. However, you may need to enforce your rights under the contract for more significant breaches, potentially leading to mediation, arbitration, or litigation. These steps can be costly and time-consuming, so solving disputes through open and honest communication is beneficial.

Effective contract management involves continuously monitoring the obligations of both parties to ensure compliance and addressing potential issues before they escalate. Regular review and contract updates can also help keep them relevant and reflect new laws or business realities.

Navigating contracts and legal agreements with the savvy of a seasoned captain ensures your LLC can sail smoothly through business dealings, fortified against potential disputes, and anchored in mutual respect and professionalism. As you continue to engage with suppliers, customers, and partners, remember that each contract is more than just a document—it's a building block in the structure of your successful business relationships.

As we close this chapter on navigating contracts and legal agreements, remember that the contracts you create and sign are not just routine paperwork; they are integral to the structure and security of your business operations. They set the stage for successful partnerships and safe business practices. In the next chapter, we'll explore how to manage your LLC effectively, focusing on strategies that ensure its growth and sustainability.

MANAGING YOUR LLC

Imagine stepping onto the deck of your very own ship; the salty breeze is invigorating as you gaze across the vast, open sea. Managing your LLC can feel quite similar—thrilling, a bit daunting, but ultimately a grand adventure where you're the captain steering your crew toward treasures untold. But, as every seasoned captain knows, smooth seas don't make skillful sailors. The ability to manage your ship, navigate through storms, and keep your crew aligned and motivated tests—and proves—your mettle.

5.1 EFFECTIVE LEADERSHIP AND MANAGEMENT TECHNIQUES FOR LLC OWNERS

Leadership Styles and Their Impact

In the diverse world of leadership, styles vary as widely as the fish in the sea. From the transformational leaders who inspire and energize their teams to achieve extraordinary things to the transactional leaders who ensure that the ship runs on a tight schedule, each style has unique benefits and challenges. As an LLC owner, identifying your primary leadership style can profoundly affect how your team performs as well as how your business ultimately fares.

Transformational leadership, for instance, is all about creating a vision and inspiring your team to embrace this vision as their own. Think of it as setting sail toward a promising, albeit distant, horizon—your crew needs to believe in the journey as much as you do. This style is particularly effective in environments where creativity and innovation are keys to success, as it encourages team members to think outside the box and be proactive in solving problems.

Transactional leadership, on the other hand, is more like navigating a well-charted sea. It focuses on routines, clear objectives, rewards, and penalties. It's about ensuring that the daily operations of your LLC run smoothly and efficiently, like a well-oiled machine. This style can be incredibly effective when precision and order are paramount or when the business is going through a turbulent phase and needs a steady hand to guide it.

Situational leadership, a dynamic and flexible style, adapts to the prevailing winds and waters. It requires you to assess the situation and adjust your leadership style accordingly. For instance, a new hire might need more hands-on guidance and encouragement (akin to coaching), while a seasoned employee might only need support from afar (more of a delegating approach).

Understanding and applying these different leadership styles can help you enhance team performance and navigate your business toward successful outcomes. It's about knowing when to inspire, when to direct, and when to delegate, ensuring your crew is motivated, productive, and happy.

Decision-Making Processes

In the world of LLC management, decision-making is the rudder that steers the ship. Effective decision-making processes promote transparency and inclusivity, making every crew member feel valued and part of the journey. One practical approach is the democratic or participative decision-making process, where team members are invited to share their opinions and vote on significant decisions. This fosters a sense of ownership among team members and leverages diverse perspectives, leading to more well-rounded and effective choices.

However, inclusivity doesn't mean every decision needs a full team meeting. Empowering employees by delegating decision-making authority can be incredibly effective for more routine decisions. It boosts morale by showing trust in their abilities and judgment, and it frees up your time to focus on steering the broader strategic goals of your LLC.

Conflict Resolution

Let's face it: Conflicts are almost inevitable when there are human interactions. Like a storm on the sea, conflicts can arise suddenly and can be damaging if not handled properly.

Effective conflict resolution strategies are essential for maintaining a professional and positive work environment. A helpful method is the "interest-based relational" approach. It focuses on the underlying reasons behind the conflict rather than the surface emotions and positions. Understanding each party's needs and interests allows you to navigate a resolution that respects everyone's concerns while maintaining strong professional relationships.

Continuous Learning and Improvement

The sea of business is ever-changing, with new technologies, trends, and regulations constantly emerging. For LLC owners and their teams, embracing continuous learning is like continuously charting your course based on the most up-to-date maps and navigational tools. Encouraging ongoing personal and professional development can keep your LLC competitive and innovative. Consider investing in workshops, classes, and resources that align with your business goals and industry trends. Additionally, fostering a culture where feedback is welcomed and acted upon can lead to continuous improvement and growth.

Encouraging your team to learn and continuously providing growth opportunities can transform your LLC from a mere vessel to a flagship of innovation and success. It's about creating an environment where every team member is equipped, encouraged, and excited to contribute their best, ensuring that your LLC reaches and surpasses its envisioned horizons.

5.2 HIRING YOUR FIRST EMPLOYEES: LEGAL AND OPERATIONAL GUIDELINES

Ah, the exciting milestone of hiring your first employee—it's a bit like deciding to grow your solo kitchen escapade into a bustling café. Suddenly, it's not just about your ability to whip up a storm but also about finding the right sous chefs who can dance to the rhythm of your entrepreneurial spirit. But before you put up that "Help Wanted" sign, let's navigate the less thrilling yet critical waters of employment laws. Ensuring your burgeoning business stays afloat in the sea of legal compliance is crucial.

Navigating employment laws begins with understanding the fundamentals, such as anti-discrimination laws. These laws, including the famous Title VII of the Civil Rights Act, ensure you're hiring based on merit, not on biases. It's all about fairness—ensuring every candidate has an equal shot at joining your team, regardless of their race, religion, gender, or any other characteristic that's not relevant to their job performance. Then, wage regulations, like the Fair Labor Standards Act (FLSA), govern minimum wage, overtime, and other critical aspects of compensation. It's the blueprint ensuring everyone gets a fair deal for their time and effort in your café. And let's not forget about workers' compensation requirements, providing benefits to your employees if they get injured on the job—a safety net that keeps everyone reassured.

With the legal framework clear, creating job descriptions and roles is your next step. This isn't just about listing responsibilities; it's about sculpting the DNA of your future workforce. Each role should align with your LLC's operational needs and goals. Think of it as crafting a recipe for each position—what ingredients do you need? There is a dash of creativity here and a spoonful of tech-savvy there. Comprehensive job descriptions help attract the right candidates and set clear expectations from the get-go, ensuring everyone knows what's on their plate.

Regarding effective recruitment strategies, diversity is your spice rack—it enhances everything. Expanding your search beyond the usual recruitment platforms can bring unexpected, rich flavors to your team. Online job postings are the bread and butter, sure, but don't underestimate the power of networking events where you can meet potential candidates in a more dynamic environment. Recruitment agencies can also be valuable allies, especially when looking for a specific blend of skills. They can sift through the candidate pool, presenting you with only those who truly fit your recipe for success.

Finally, once you've found your ideal candidates, you bring them into your café's family through the onboarding and training process. This isn't just about showing them where the coffee beans are stored or how the register works; it's about integrating them into the culture and workflow of your business. A step-by-step onboarding guide helps new hires understand their roles and responsibilities and aligns them with your business's values and goals. Regular training sessions keep their skills sharp and engagement high—essential ingredients for a thriving business.

Navigating these aspects of hiring and managing employees may seem daunting. Still, with a clear understanding of the legal requirements and a strategic approach to recruitment and onboarding, you'll not only build a team that's capable and compliant but also one that shares your vision and passion for the business. It's about setting the stage for a collective success story, where every member plays a crucial part in turning your entrepreneurial dreams into delectable reality. This approach ensures that your first foray into expanding your team lays the groundwork for a robust, vibrant, and compliant workforce ready to take your business to new heights.

5.3 DEVELOPING A STRONG BRAND IDENTITY FOR YOUR LLC

Think of your LLC's brand as its heartbeat, a unique rhythm that resonates with your customers and sets the tempo for your business's interactions in the market. Defining your brand is like tuning a guitar; each string must resonate perfectly to create harmony. Your brand's mission, vision, and values are these strings. They define your business's existence, its goals, and its guiding principles. Imagine you're crafting a craft brewery. Your mission could be to revolutionize the local beer scene with innovative, community-sourced flavors. Your vision might be to become a staple in local bars and homes, and your values could center on sustainability and community involvement. This clear articulation helps align your internal strategies. It communicates to your customers what your brand stands for, making your brewery about more than just beer—it's a unique cultural contribution.

Transitioning from the why to the how we delve into your visual identity—this is your brand's attire and how it presents itself to the world. Elements like your logo, color schemes, and typography are not merely aesthetic choices; they communicate your brand's personality. Think about the logo for your brewery: perhaps a vibrant hop intertwined with a local landmark, signaling both your focus on craft brews and your community roots. Choosing colors and fonts that reflect the spirit of your brand—maybe earth tones to signify sustainability and a bold, modern font to mirror innovation—helps forge a visual connection with your audience. These elements should consistently reflect the essence of your brand, whether on a beer label, your website, or promotional materials, ensuring that your brewery is instantly recognizable and memorable.

Crafting compelling brand messaging is like storytelling; every advertisement, product description, and social media post tells a part of your story. It's about weaving the elements of your mission, vision, and values into messages that inform, engage, and inspire your audience. Consider the story of a special brew made entirely from locally sourced ingredients, each bottle sold contributing to local environmental efforts. This message does more than sell beer; it tells a story of community impact, aligning with your values and resonating with like-minded customers who are not just buying a product but participating in a cause.

Maintaining consistency across all channels is crucial; it's like ensuring every musician in an orchestra is playing in tune with the others. Whether your customers browse your website, read a flyer, or scroll through your social media, their experience should feel cohesive and seamless. This consistency builds trust and recognition, making your brand feel reliable and professional. For your brewery, your innovative, community-focused brand identity should be palpable in every interaction, from the design of your website to the tone of your tweets. It's about ensuring every touchpoint reinforces your brand's unique identity, turning casual customers into loyal advocates.

Navigating through these aspects of brand development might seem daunting. Still, each step you take in defining and expressing your brand identity solidifies your market position and enhances your connection with customers. Like crafting a fine brew, it requires attention to detail, consistency, and a commitment to quality. As you continue to develop and refine your brand, remember that it is the beacon that guides your business, illuminating your path in the marketplace and drawing people not just to your products but to your vision and values.

5.4 STRATEGIC MARKETING FOR LLC GROWTH

Embarking on developing a strategic marketing plan can feel akin to sketching a treasure map. It's not just about marking the spot where the gold lies but charting a path to navigate uncharted waters, ensuring that each step brings you closer to your bounty. As an LLC owner, this journey begins with thorough market research. Dive into understanding who your customers are, what they need, and what they currently enjoy. This phase is about listening, observing, and gathering valuable insights that will guide every marketing move you make. Equally important is a competitive analysis—knowing your rivals' strengths and weaknesses can help you carve a niche for your brand or exploit gaps in their offerings.

With this intelligence in your arsenal, you can set targeted marketing goals. These aren't just aspirations but measurable, specific objectives that align with your business's overall strategy—for instance, increasing website traffic by 30% within six months or boosting customer retention by 20% by the end of the year. These goals should act as benchmarks for success and as lighthouses guiding your marketing efforts, ensuring they are focused and structured.

Transitioning from planning to execution, cost-effective marketing strategies are your best allies, especially when resources are limited. Social media marketing, for instance, offers a fertile playground for small businesses. Platforms like Instagram, Facebook, and X (formerly known as Twitter) provide tools to reach a broad audience without the hefty price tag of traditional advertising. Content marketing, including blogs, e-books, and videos, allows you to share valuable information that resonates with your audience, establishing your brand as a trustworthy authority in your field. Meanwhile, email campaigns can be a direct line to your customers, providing personalized interactions that foster strong relationships and encourage loyalty. Each of these strategies requires creativity and persistence, but when executed well, they can yield substantial returns without draining your coffers.

Measuring the success of these efforts is crucial. Launching a marketing campaign is not enough; you must know how it performs. Utilize metrics and analytics to track engagement, conversion rates, and overall return on investment. Tools like Google Analytics for web traffic, social media insights for engagement and reach, and email marketing software for open rates and conversions can clearly show what's working and what's not. This data isn't just numbers on a screen; it's the feedback from the market, telling you if you're on the right path or if adjustments are needed.

Lastly, the ability to adapt to market changes and customer feedback is what keeps your marketing strategy relevant and effective. The market is a living entity, constantly evolving with new trends, technologies, and customer preferences. Stay agile and ready to tweak your strategies based on the data. For example, if a particular type of content resonates well with your audience, consider doubling down on it. Conversely, if a marketing channel isn't delivering results, it might be time to pivot and try new avenues. This flexibility doesn't just help optimize resources; it ensures that your marketing efforts align with what your customers want and need, keeping your brand resonant and relevant in a competitive landscape.

Navigating through these facets of strategic marketing requires creativity, analytical thinking, and resilience. It's about setting a course, following the stars of data and feedback, and being prepared to adjust the sails when the winds change. With a solid marketing plan in place and a commitment to adapt and evolve, your LLC can reach its current customers more effectively and discover new growth opportunities.

5.5 SCALING YOUR BUSINESS: WHEN AND HOW TO EXPAND

Scaling your business isn't just about having more; it's about *being* more. It's a thrilling phrase that says, "Hey, we've done something right!" But it also whispers, "Are we ready for the next big leap?" Identifying when your LLC is ripe for scaling is like knowing exactly when your homemade loaf is ready to come out of the oven—too soon and it's doughy, too late and it's overdone. Consistent profits are a clear indicator; they're like the golden crust on your bread, showing you that your business model isn't just working; it's thriving. Strong customer demand, where you see more "hungry" customers than you can currently "feed," and operational stability, where your day-to-day processes run smoothly without your constant oversight, are also tell-tale signs that your business might be ready to expand.

Now, let's talk expansion strategies. It's akin to deciding whether to bake more loaves, experiment with new recipes, or open a new bakery in a neighboring town. Diversification, for instance, can mean adding new products or services that complement your existing offerings. It's a great way to attract different customers and reduce the risks associated with relying on a single product line. On the other hand, franchising involves duplicating your successful business model and letting others run similar operations under your brand. It can rapidly expand your business footprint without you having to manage new locations directly. Then there's the option of entering new markets, even international ones, which involve significant research and adaptation to meet local tastes and regulatory requirements but can also open up substantial new customer bases.

Each of these strategies has its charms and challenges, and the right choice depends heavily on your business's strengths and the market conditions. It's like choosing the right tool for a job—using a hammer when you need a screwdriver can end up causing more damage than good. Assess your LLC's unique capabilities and market opportunities to determine which strategy aligns best with your long-term goals.

However, with great expansion comes great responsibility, and managing the risks associated with scaling is crucial. It's not unlike ensuring your entire crew knows how to handle the sails before heading into stormier seas. Careful planning is your compass here; it involves forecasting financial impacts, understanding the increased operational demands, and preparing for potential market shifts. Gradual expansion can be safer, allowing you to test the waters with minimal risk before diving headfirst. Securing adequate funding is also critical; it ensures you have the resources to support your growth while maintaining your existing operations.

Sustaining growth post-expansion requires continuous innovation and adaptation. The market is a sea of changing currents and winds, and what worked yesterday may not work tomorrow. Keep a keen eye on industry trends and evolving customer preferences. Strategic partnerships can also propel your growth by combining strengths, resources, and market reach. Ongoing market research also plays a pivotal role; it helps you stay ahead of the curve, ensuring your business grows and thrives in the new territories it explores.

In essence, scaling your business is about carefully balancing the excitement of growth with the realities of larger operational scopes and market complexities. It's about ensuring that your business remains as responsive and innovative as it was when you first dreamed it up. As you consider expanding your LLC, keep these insights in mind and approach each decision with enthusiasm and strategic foresight, ready to take on new challenges and seize new opportunities.

MAKING LLCS ACCESSIBLE TO EVERYONE

"Knowledge is like money: to be of value it must circulate, and in circulating it can increase in quantity and, hopefully, in value."

— LOUIS L'AMOUR

For me, taking the LLC route is a no-brainer. The advantages it offers are significant, and a well-structured LLC can offer immense protection and potential to a new business. For many people, though, the mere sight of the reams of jargon associated with setting up an LLC is enough to leave them running in the opposite direction, and many entrepreneurs don't even get as far as discovering the benefits, let alone starting the process. Having seen so many businesses enjoy huge success by taking the LLC approach, it's my goal to change this and demystify the whole process. That's how it is that you come to be reading this now – I made it my goal to make LLCs accessible through this book.

I have quite a mission on my hands though: How do I reach more people and make them aware that the process of setting up an LLC is easier than they think? The guidance is here, but how does it reach the people who need it? There's an answer to this question, and this is where I have to rope you in too: The answer is *reviews*.

The reason people shy away from setting up an LLC is because they're intimidated by the amount of work involved and the amount of complex jargon that surrounds it. When real, relatable people who are working through the same things that they start spreading the word and showing them that it can be done, they're much more likely to read up on the process and take the leap themselves. If you would be willing to leave a short review online, you'll take the headache out of this for so many more business owners.

By leaving a review of this book on Amazon, you'll help anyone looking for guidance about setting up an LLC to see exactly where they can find it.

Reviews help to connect books with the readers who are looking for them, and with your assistance, I can help more businesses benefit from setting up an LLC.

Thank you for your support. A review might not seem like much, but it's an incredibly powerful tool when it comes to sharing information.

ADVANCED TAX STRATEGIES

Imagine yourself as a treasure hunter standing on the brink of unearthing a hidden fortune, not with a shovel on a deserted island but right within the financial statements of your LLC. Navigating the labyrinth of tax deductions and credits is like deciphering an ancient map, each line and symbol guiding you to fiscal treasures that can significantly boost your LLC's profitability. As you delve into this chapter, consider each tax deduction and credit as a piece of gold, mastering them as the art of keeping more of your hard-earned money. Let's embark on this treasure hunt together, shall we?

6.1 ADVANCED TAX DEDUCTIONS AND CREDITS FOR LLCS

Identifying Eligible Deductions

One of tax strategy's most exhilarating aspects is discovering deductions you can claim. It's akin to finding hidden doors in a room you thought you knew well. Standard deductions for LLCs include home office expenses, travel costs, and equipment purchases—each capable of substantially reducing your taxable income.

Let's start with the home office deduction, ideal for those who stir the pots of their business magic right from their living room or a dedicated office space at home. The key is understanding the IRS's definition of a "regular and exclusive" use area. It doesn't mean your home office can double as a guest room or a sporadic movie lounge. It's your business fortress and calculating its deduction can be done using the simplified option (a standard deduction based on the square footage of your office) or the regular method (deducting actual expenses). Both methods have charm, like choosing between a flat rate for treasure or appraising each jewel individually.

Travel expenses present another lucrative deduction area, especially when jet-setting around the country to expand your empire. Whether it's airfare, lodging, or even meals during your business travels, these costs can be deducted, provided they are ordinary, necessary, and directly related to your business. Imagine each trip as a quest for new business opportunities—every expense is a stepping stone toward potential profits.

Equipment purchases, from computers to company cars, can significantly lower your tax bill through depreciation deductions. This allows you to deduct the cost of tangible property over the expected life of the equipment, turning a hefty purchase into a series of smaller, digestible tax breaks spread over several years. It's like turning a chest of gold into a steady stream of financial support for your business adventures.

Leveraging Tax Credits

While deductions reduce the amount of income subject to tax, credits reduce your tax bill directly, dollar for dollar, making them incredibly potent tools in your tax-saving arsenal. For instance, the Work Opportunity Tax Credit (WOTC) rewards you for hiring individuals from certain groups who face significant barriers to employment. Each eligible hire can translate into a tax credit of up to $9,600, depending on the employee's category and the wages paid. It's as if the government is co-sponsoring your crew of business buccaneers.

Additionally, for the eco-conscious LLCs, embracing green technologies isn't just good for the planet—it's financially savvy too. Energy efficiency credits can be claimed for everything from installing solar panels to undertaking environmentally friendly renovations. It's a scenario where being kind to Earth enriches your coffers.

Documentation and Record Keeping

The thrill of discovering these deductions and credits, however, comes with the meticulous responsibility of documentation. Just as a treasure hunter wouldn't venture without a map, you shouldn't navigate tax deductions without thorough record-keeping. This includes keeping detailed logs of travel dates, purposes, and expenses, receipts for equipment purchases, and employment records qualifying for the WOTC.

Effective organization strategies—such as using digital tools for scanning and storing receipts or employing dedicated accounting software—can transform the potentially arduous task of documentation into a manageable part of your business routine. Think of it as cataloging your treasures; the better your system, the easier it is to claim your rightful rewards.

Case Studies

Consider the case of EcoDesigns LLC, a small business specializing in sustainable home decor. By meticulously documenting their expenses on energy-efficient equipment and renovations, they maximized their eligible deductions and secured sizable energy efficiency credits. Over the fiscal year, this strategic approach resulted in a 30% reduction in their taxable income, illustrating the profound impact of well-leveraged tax strategies.

Similarly, TechTutors LLC, which hired several veterans facing employment challenges, utilized the WOTC to offset a significant portion of their tax liabilities. The documentation of their hiring practices and the subsequent tax credits supported their community and enhanced their financial sustainability.

In both scenarios, the LLCs turned potential tax burdens into opportunities for growth and community impact, showcasing the dual benefits of strategic tax planning and conscientious record-keeping. As you chart your course through the complex waters of LLC taxation, remember that with the proper knowledge and tools, the world of tax deductions and credits can be both navigable and richly rewarding.

6.2 HANDLING PAYROLL TAXES FOR YOUR EMPLOYEES

Navigating the intricacies of payroll taxes can sometimes feel like you're trying to solve a Rubik's cube—twist one way, and you think you're close to solving it, but then you realize a whole other layer needs aligning. Understanding the obligations of payroll taxes is foundational for maintaining the financial health of your LLC and staying compliant with various tax authorities. As an LLC that employs staff, you're responsible for paying out salaries and withholding the correct amounts for federal, state, and local taxes from these salaries. This includes withholding income taxes and contributing to Social Security and Medicare, collectively known as Federal Insurance Contributions Act (FICA) taxes. Each payment period, you hold back a portion of your employee's earnings and then remit these withholdings to the appropriate tax agencies, acting somewhat like a tax collector.

Thus, setting up an efficient payroll system is crucial. It's like setting up a kitchen that makes cooking complex meals more manageable. You have two main paths: managing payroll in-house or outsourcing it to a third-party provider. If you choose the in-house route, you must be prepared to invest in good payroll software, which automates most of the grunt work. This software can calculate wages, withhold the correct tax amounts, and even handle filings and payments to tax agencies. The DIY approach might save you money and give you more control, but it requires a solid understanding of payroll regulations and meticulous attention to detail.

Conversely, outsourcing payroll to third-party providers can be like hiring a gourmet chef for your kitchen. It's more expensive, but it buys you peace of mind. These providers are experts in navigating the complexities of payroll taxes and will handle most of the process for you, from calculating taxes to filing returns. This can be particularly beneficial if your LLC operates in multiple states, each with its own set of payroll rules and regulations. The key here is to choose a provider that fits your budget and scales with your business as it grows.

Now, even with the best systems in place, mistakes can happen, which can be costly in payroll taxes. One common error is misclassifying employees as independent contractors. This mistake can lead to significant liabilities, including back taxes and penalties because different tax rules apply to contractors. Ensure you understand the criteria that differentiate an employee from a contractor—think about it like distinguishing between a freelancer who occasionally decorates your bakery's cakes and a full-time baker who works the ovens every day.

Another frequent misstep is failing to keep accurate records. Imagine trying to bake a cake a year after you first tested the recipe, but you scribbled the ingredients on a napkin that's since been lost. Without precise records of how much you've paid each employee and what taxes you've withheld, you could be under the microscope of a tax audit with little to defend your practices. To avoid such pitfalls, maintain detailed records of all payroll activities and regularly review your payroll reports to catch and rectify any discrepancies quickly.

Utilizing Payroll Software

In the digital age, leveraging technology can significantly streamline your payroll processes. Paying for good payroll software is not just an expense; it's an investment in accuracy and efficiency. These systems automate almost every aspect of payroll, from entering employee hours to filing tax forms. They reduce the likelihood of human error and save you a mountain of time. Features like automatic tax calculations, electronic filings, and seamless integration with your accounting systems can transform a tangled mess of payroll tasks into a smooth, well-oiled machine.

When choosing payroll software, consider its compatibility with your existing systems, its ability to scale as your business grows, and the level of customer support provided. Consider choosing a vehicle: You want something reliable that fits your current needs but can also handle a future where you might decide to expand. The right software not only keeps you compliant with tax laws but also provides valuable insights into your labor costs, helping you make smarter financial decisions for your business.

As you weave through the complexities of payroll taxes and systems, remember that each step you take toward optimizing this aspect of your business notates your commitment to your team and your enterprise's integrity. It's about building a framework supporting your business's compliance with the law and overall financial health.

6.3 YEAR-END TAX PLANNING TIPS FOR LLCS

Navigating the fiscal waters at the end of the year can often feel like you're trying to tie up a boat in a storm. It's all about securing your financials in such a way that you minimize your tax liabilities and maximize returns. One of the most effective maneuvers in this regard is the strategic deferral of income. Now, you might wonder, why push income to the next year? It's like asking your dinner guests to arrive later so you have extra time to whip up a dessert that could use more chilling. By delaying specific invoices or the receipt of payments until after December 31, you effectively reduce the income recorded for the current fiscal year, thus lowering your immediate tax liability.

This tactic requires a good sense of timing and balance. For instance, if you anticipate higher revenue or tax rate increases next year, there might be better moves than pushing income forward. However, delaying income is a savvy strategy if the next year brings opportunities for higher deductions or you expect to be in a lower tax bracket. Working closely with your accountant to forecast these variables accurately is crucial. Think of it as planning your route through foggy waters; without a sound navigation system and a clear understanding of the upcoming conditions, you might find yourself off course.

Now, let's talk about accelerating expenses. This strategy involves making advance payments for rent, supplies, or business services before the year ends to increase your deductions for the current tax year. Imagine you're hosting a huge New Year's bash—it would make sense to buy all your party supplies in December rather than January to take advantage of the festive discounts, right? Similarly, by prepaying expenses, you ensure that your business is well-stocked for the coming months and lower your taxable income for the current year. This could include stocking up on office supplies, prepaying insurance premiums, or making advance payments to contractors.

Shifting gears to retirement contributions is a way to secure your future and an intelligent tax-reduction strategy. Contributions to plans like a Simplified Employee Pension (SEP) individual retirement account (IRA) or a solo 401(k) can be deducted from your current year's income, reducing your taxable income. These plans offer you a nest egg for the future and provide current financial benefits. For example, in 2023, you can contribute up to 25% of your compensation or a maximum of $61,000 to a SEP IRA. It's like putting money into a high-yield savings jar that prepares you for retirement and gives you a tax break today.

Lastly, let's unwrap the potential of charitable contributions. If your LLC has had a prosperous year, considering giving back can do more than make you feel good. Charitable contributions made through your LLC can reduce your taxable income. However, ensuring that the IRS recognizes the organizations you choose to qualify for these deductions is essential. Also, keeping thorough records of such donations is crucial. It's like maintaining receipts from your holiday shopping; you need them handy for returns or exchanges. Here, you keep them handy for tax filings. Engaging in philanthropy bolsters your business's community standing and provides tangible fiscal benefits.

Navigating these year-end tax planning strategies effectively requires a blend of foresight, timing, and, sometimes, a bit of boldness. By understanding and utilizing these tactics, you position your LLC to weather the fiscal storms and sail smoothly into a prosperous new year. As you consider these strategies, engage with your financial advisor to tailor them to your specific business scenario, ensuring that each decision is informed and aligned with your broader economic goals. Remember, good tax planning is much like good navigation—it doesn't just help you avoid pitfalls; it sets you on the course for future success.

6.4 NAVIGATING AUDITS AND LEGAL TAX ISSUES

Imagine you're on stage, the spotlight's on you, and it's time for your solo. That's what facing a tax audit feels like: daunting, yes, but also a chance to show you've got everything in harmony. Audits are about more than finding mistakes; they are about ensuring everything is well-tuned to the tax laws.

Like any other business entity, LLCs can sometimes hit a sour note that calls for an auditor's attention. Common triggers for these audits include claiming significant losses that might seem out of tune with your reported income, excessive deductions that appear more ambitious than your revenue might justify, or discrepancies that suggest your lifestyle could be more in sync with what your tax returns report. These discrepancies can make the IRS or other tax authorities curious if there's more to your financial story.

If an audit letter hits your mailbox, consider it a call to go backstage and ensure every part of your performance is ready for review. Preparing for an audit involves gathering your financial scripts—everything from receipts and invoices to bank statements and previous tax returns. This documentation is your setlist, proving each number you've performed over the years. These documents must be organized and easily accessible, which speaks volumes about your business's credibility and can significantly simplify the audit process. Understanding your rights in this scenario is also crucial. You have the right to know why you're being audited, what documents you must provide, and, if necessary, seek professional representation. This could be a tax attorney or a CPA who knows the tax tunes well and can conduct the orchestra on your behalf, ensuring that your rights are upheld and your case is presented clearly and effectively.

The audit process can vary in length and complexity, depending on what's under review. You might face a simple correspondence audit, where you'll need to mail in the requested documents, or it could be a field audit, where auditors visit your business. During these interactions, staying composed and cooperative is vital. Present your documentation clearly and answer questions with the confidence of someone who knows their part well. If you disagree with an auditor's finding, it's like hitting a wrong note—you must know how to correct it swiftly and accurately. This is where having professional representation can help; they can articulate the nuances of your financial practices and negotiate with the tax authorities effectively.

But what if the final curtain falls and you find the audit results aren't in your favor? The tax world encore involves legal recourse and appeals. You have the right to challenge the audit's outcome if you believe it's incorrect. Filing an appeal can be seen as requesting a review of your last performance, ensuring every note and every rhythm was judged correctly. This part of the process can be intricate and warrants professional advice. Tax attorneys or CPAs can help you navigate the appeal, preparing a solid case to present before the tax tribunal or court.

Handling an audit is no small task, but with the proper preparation and support, it's a part of the business symphony you can get through. Keeping your records meticulous, understanding your rights, and knowing when to bring in the experts can transform this challenging solo into a harmonious part of your business journey. Remember, audits aren't just about scrutiny—they're opportunities to prove your business's financial integrity and commitment to compliance.

6.5 INNOVATIVE ACCOUNTING SOLUTIONS FOR MODERN LLCS

In the fast-evolving landscape of business technology, staying ahead isn't just about keeping pace; it's about setting the pace. This is where cloud-based accounting platforms come into play, transforming how modern LLCs manage their finances. Imagine accessing your financial data from anywhere, at any time—whether you're sipping espresso in a Parisian café or catching some rays on a beach in Bali. Cloud-based accounting provides this level of accessibility, ensuring that your financial operations don't tie you down to a desk. Real-time financial reporting means you can see up-to-the-minute results of your business activities. This allows for quicker decision-making and a more agile response to market changes, like a chef who tastes the soup continuously and tweaks the seasoning to perfection throughout the cooking process.

The scalability of cloud-based platforms is another game-changer. As your business grows from a solo operation to a bustling enterprise, your accounting system can expand alongside it without costly hardware upgrades or disruptive system migrations. It's akin to a building with expandable walls that adjust as more space is needed. Whether adding new products, services, or whole new branches to your business tree, cloud-based systems grow with you, ensuring that your financial infrastructure stays within your business ambitions.

Now, let's talk automation—every entrepreneur's dream. Automation tools within these platforms can handle everything from invoicing and expense tracking to financial reporting and payroll. They work tirelessly in the background like diligent elves, ensuring every number is crunched accurately and every penny is accounted for. This minimizes human errors—a typical villain in the accounting world—and frees up your time. Time that you can invest back into strategizing for growth, exploring new markets, or simply enjoying the entrepreneurial journey a little more.

Integration With Other Business Tools

Your accounting software should not be an isolated island in today's interconnected digital ecosystem. Integration capabilities allow your accounting system to talk seamlessly with other tools you use, such as customer relationship management (CRM) systems, e-commerce platforms, or even inventory management software. This interconnectedness ensures that data flows smoothly between systems, reducing the need for manual data entry and the errors that come with it. For instance, a sale recorded in your e-commerce platform can automatically update your inventory and financial records, keeping everything in sync. Like a well-rehearsed orchestra, every part works in perfect harmony, providing deeper insights into your financial performance and business health.

Imagine the enhanced customer insights you can gain when your CRM is integrated with your accounting software. You can track customer behavior from the first point of contact to the final sale and beyond, tailoring your marketing and sales strategies to maximize profitability. This kind of integrated approach doesn't just add efficiency; it adds intelligence to your operations, turning raw data into actionable insights.

Future Trends in Accounting Technology

Looking ahead, the horizon of accounting technology is vibrant with potential. Artificial intelligence (AI) is set to play a significant role, with systems that can analyze vast amounts of data to offer predictions and insights that go beyond human capabilities. AI-driven analytics can forecast cash flow trends, identify financial bottlenecks before they become problematic, and suggest the most tax-efficient ways to manage your capital. It's like having a financial oracle in your team, one that helps you navigate the future with confidence.

Blockchain technology is another frontier. Known for its robust security features, it offers a way to process transactions with unparalleled safety, reducing the risks of fraud and cyber-attacks. In an era where digital security is more crucial than ever, integrating blockchain into your accounting processes could be akin to installing the most advanced locking mechanisms to protect your treasure trove of financial data.

As these technologies evolve, they promise to streamline and revolutionize accounting practices. By staying informed and adaptable, you can ensure that your LLC remains at the cutting edge, leveraging these innovations for enhanced efficiency, accuracy, and security.

In wrapping up this exploration of innovative accounting solutions, remember that embracing these technologies can significantly elevate your business's operational efficiency and strategic insight. From cloud-based platforms offering flexibility and scalability to AI and blockchain transforming data security and financial analysis, the future of accounting is here. As you integrate these tools into your business practices, you're not just keeping up with the times; you're driving forward, ready to meet tomorrow's challenges with today's innovations. As we pivot to the next chapter, let's carry forward this spirit of innovation and readiness, exploring how these advanced tools can be further harnessed to sculpt a thriving, resilient business landscape.

TROUBLESHOOTING COMMON LLC ISSUES

Imagine your LLC as a band you've painstakingly put together. Each member plays a unique instrument, contributing to the harmonious melodies that represent your business's success. But what happens when the drummer and the guitarist are out of sync, threatening to turn your smooth tunes into discordant noise? Disputes among LLC members can be just as jarring, and if not addressed properly, they can escalate to threaten the very essence of your business ensemble.

7.1 RESOLVING DISPUTES AMONG LLC MEMBERS

Preventive Measures

Just as a band might have a setlist that guides their performances, your LLC needs a clear and comprehensive operating agreement. This document isn't just bureaucratic paperwork; think of it as the rhythm section of your band—

it keeps everyone in sync and lays down the groove for how the LLC operates. A well-drafted operating agreement includes dispute resolution processes that act like music sheets, guiding what happens when disagreements arise. They ensure that every member knows the steps to follow, reducing the chances for disputes to escalate into full-blown conflicts. It's about setting expectations right from the start, which helps maintain harmony and ensures that each member feels secure knowing there's a process to handle disagreements.

Mediation and Arbitration

Now, even with the best preparations, disputes can still arise. When they do, think of mediation and arbitration as your LLC's sound engineers, working behind the scenes to tweak the mix and balance the acoustics. These methods serve as less confrontational alternatives to court litigation and can effectively preserve business relationships. Mediation involves a neutral third-party facilitator who helps all members communicate their views and work toward a voluntary agreement. It's like having a band manager who helps each member voice their concerns and find common ground.

Arbitration, on the other hand, is a bit more structured. It's similar to bringing in a guest conductor to interpret your music sheet (operating agreement) and make decisions that help retune your band. While the arbitrator's decision is usually binding, the process is generally faster and less formal than court proceedings, allowing you to get back to making music much quicker.

Role of a Neutral Facilitator

Whether it's a mediator in the mediation process or an arbitrator in arbitration, the role of a neutral facilitator cannot be overstated. Think of this person as a guest artist who steps into your band temporarily, bringing a fresh perspective that can help bridge gaps and smooth tensions. Their neutrality ensures that no member's interests dominate the others, and their expertise in negotiation can often lead to innovative solutions that the members might not have considered. They help keep the discussions focused and productive, steering clear of the emotional whirlpools that sometimes consume business disputes.

Legal Options

Legal action may become necessary if all else fails and the internal processes do not resolve the disputes. Venturing into this territory is like taking your band to a battle of the bands—it's public, can be competitive, and has high stakes. Legal action can significantly affect your LLC, from financial costs to potential impacts on your business's reputation. Considering these implications carefully and weighing them against the potential benefits of resolving the dispute is essential. This step might sometimes be necessary to protect the business or ensure fair treatment for all members. However, it's generally seen as a last resort, used only when other, less aggressive methods have failed.

Navigating member disputes in an LLC can be as complex and nuanced as composing a symphony. Each step, from drafting a detailed operating agreement to considering legal action, plays a crucial role in maintaining the harmony and success of your business. By implementing effective dispute-resolution processes and being prepared to engage neutral facilitators, you can ensure that disagreements among members are resolved in a manner that protects both the individual interests and the overarching goals of the LLC. Remember, the goal is to make music, not war. By addressing disputes thoughtfully and proactively, you can keep your band playing harmoniously, ready to take on the world's stages.

7.2 REVIVING AN LLC IN POOR STANDING

Imagine your LLC as a once-thriving garden that's started to show signs of neglect. Perhaps the flowers aren't blooming as brightly, or the leaves have begun to yellow. Something's amiss, and it's time to get your green thumbs dirty to revive the lushness it once boasted. Similarly, when your LLC falls into poor standing, it's crucial to dig deep, uncover the root causes, and nurture it back to health. This isn't just about avoiding penalties or the threat of dissolution; it's about restoring the vitality and credibility of your business.

Identifying the Cause

The first step in this revitalization process is conducting an internal audit—thoroughly examining your business practices, compliance records, and financial obligations. Think of this as doing a complete health check-up on your LLC. You're looking for signs of noncompliance, such as missed annual filings or unpaid taxes, which can often be the culprits behind an LLC's poor standing. This step requires honesty and meticulousness. You must review financial statements, check state filing histories, and ensure all tax obligations are transparent. Sometimes, the issues are apparent, like an overlooked filing; other times, they might be buried deeper, like an error in your tax calculations.

Gathering this information can feel daunting, akin to sorting through years of family photos to organize them into albums. However, just as with photos, the picture becomes more apparent once you sort and understand what you have. You begin to see patterns—perhaps a habit of filing taxes at the last minute or neglecting to update your registered agent information. Recognizing these patterns is the first step toward making meaningful changes.

Restoring Compliance

Once you've identified the reasons behind your LLC's poor standing, the next step is to address these issues head-on. This involves filing overdue reports and resolving outstanding liabilities with state agencies and the IRS. It's like pulling weeds and planting new seeds in your garden. If you've missed annual reports, gather the necessary information and file them as soon as possible, even if late. If there are unpaid taxes, set up a payment plan or pay them in full if feasible.

This phase might also involve communicating with state agencies or tax authorities to clarify any confusion or to negotiate penalties. It's important here to be proactive and transparent. Think of it as rebuilding a fence in your garden that was knocked down in a storm—you want to ensure it's more robust this time.

Rebuilding Reputation

With compliance restored, the next task is to rebuild your LLC's reputation. This involves clear and transparent communication with all stakeholders—investors, partners, customers, and even your employees. Let them know your steps to resolve the issues and what you're doing to prevent future problems. This might include regular updates via newsletters, direct meetings, or even public statements if the situation warrants it.

Think of this as restoring trust in a personal relationship. It's not just about saying you've changed; it's about showing it through consistent actions. Perhaps you can implement a new compliance monitoring system or schedule regular financial audits. These actions speak volumes about your commitment to maintaining good standing and can significantly enhance your credibility and trustworthiness in the eyes of all who interact with your LLC.

Monitoring and Prevention

Finally, to prevent future lapses, set up ongoing monitoring systems. This is the equivalent of installing a drip irrigation system in your garden to ensure your plants receive consistent, adequate water. For your LLC, it might involve quarterly reviews of your compliance status or regular check-ins with a legal advisor to ensure all new regulations are being met.

Implementing robust internal controls is also crucial. These can include automated reminders for filing deadlines, regular training sessions for your team on compliance matters, and a clear escalation path for any issues that might arise. Think of these measures as the trellises and supports in your garden—they help everything grow upright and strong, reducing the risk of problems reoccurring.

By taking these steps—identifying the cause of noncompliance, restoring compliance, rebuilding reputation, and setting up systems to prevent future issues—you can revive your LLC's standing and ensure it remains healthy and flourishing. Like turning a neglected garden into a haven of growth and beauty, this process requires effort, persistence, and care, but the results—a robust, compliant, and respected LLC—are well worth it.

7.3 DEALING WITH A FINANCIAL CRISIS IN AN LLC SETUP

Navigating through a financial crisis in your LLC can feel like trying to steer a boat through a storm with a broken rudder. The waves are high, the wind is strong, and every decision could be the tipping point. Recognizing the early warning signs that your LLC is entering choppy financial waters is crucial. These signs often manifest as cash flow issues, such as struggling to cover basic operational costs or delays in paying suppliers. You might also notice a sudden drop in sales due to a new competitor or a decrease in market demand. Or it could be the increasing debt levels, where your business relies more on credit to stay afloat. Think of these signs as the dark clouds on the horizon— foreboding, yes, but also a crucial warning that allows you to prepare.

Once you've spotted these signs, crafting a crisis management plan becomes your next essential step. This isn't about panicking and throwing everything overboard. It's about carefully deciding which payments are crucial to keep your LLC alive and which can be delayed. Prioritizing payments to creditors is a delicate dance. You must maintain good relationships with suppliers essential to your operation while possibly negotiating longer payment terms. At the same time, exploring emergency funding options can provide the lifeline you need. This might involve opening a line of credit, securing a short-term loan, or contacting investors for additional capital. Each option carries its own risks and benefits, like choosing whether to batten down the hatches or attempt to ride out the storm.

Cost reduction techniques also play a critical role in stabilizing your LLC's finances without compromising the quality of your products or services. This is not about slashing and burning your way through the budget but brilliant, strategic cuts. Perhaps it's renegotiating rent or utility expenses or streamlining your operations to reduce waste. For example, if you own a café, could you adjust your opening hours to times when customer traffic is highest? Or, if you run a delivery service, could optimizing your routes save on fuel costs? These decisions require a keen understanding of your business's core needs and capabilities— what must be maintained to keep the doors open and what can be trimmed, even temporarily.

When the financial waters are particularly murky, seeking professional help can be your beacon. Financial advisors, restructuring specialists, or bankruptcy attorneys have the expertise to navigate these treacherous conditions. They can provide a detailed analysis of your financial situation, help restructure your debt, or guide you through complex scenarios like restructuring under bankruptcy protection. Engaging with these professionals should be seen not as a last resort but as a proactive step toward recovery. It's about admitting that sometimes, steering the ship on your own is not enough and that the guidance of seasoned navigators can make all the difference in safely reaching calmer waters.

Navigating a financial crisis requires courage, decisiveness, and, sometimes, the humility to seek help. You can steer your LLC through the stormiest seas by recognizing the early warning signs, developing a robust crisis management plan, implementing effective cost-cutting measures, and not hesitating to consult financial experts. Remember, the goal is not just to survive the storm but to emerge more robust, ready to sail forward with renewed vigor and insight.

7.4 EXIT STRATEGIES FOR LLC OWNERS

Deciding to exit your LLC is like closing a beloved book you've spent years writing. It's filled with chapters of hard work, unexpected plot twists, and invaluable lessons. Understanding your exit strategies is crucial whether you're considering turning the page due to retirement, pursuing new adventures, or simply because it's time for a change. It's not just about stepping away; it's about ensuring the story of your business continues to thrive, or if it must end, it does so gracefully.

When contemplating your exit, you have several paths you could take, each with its own set of considerations. Selling the business is a standard route, offering a potentially lucrative end to your hard work. It's like passing on a novel to another enthusiastic author who can continue the story. Alternatively, transferring ownership to a partner or a trusted employee can preserve the business's legacy, like handing over a family heirloom to someone who understands its value and history. Sometimes, liquidating assets—selling off the business's properties and inventory—might be the most practical option, especially if continuing the company isn't feasible.

Determining a fair valuation for your LLC is similar to pricing a piece of art you've created; it requires a deep understanding of its worth. Several methods can help you establish this value. Asset-based approaches consider the company's total net assets—this is straightforward but might undervalue ongoing profitable operations. Using earnings multiples involves multiplying the business's profits by a factor typical for the industry, which can highlight the business's earning potential to prospective buyers. Market valuation techniques, where you compare your business to similar ones recently sold, can also provide realistic figures. Each method has nuances; often, a combination of these approaches is used to arrive at the most equitable valuation.

Your business acumen truly comes into play when negotiating the sale or transfer of your LLC. It's crucial to protect your interests and ensure the transition is smooth. Start by preparing a comprehensive information packet for potential buyers or successors, which includes financial statements, client information, and a summary of business operations. This transparency builds trust and helps the other party understand precisely what they are getting into. When discussions begin, remember that negotiation is a two-way street; it's about finding a win-win situation where both sides feel satisfied. Be prepared to make concessions but also know your nonnegotiables, those aspects of the deal you are unwilling to compromise on.

Lastly, the legal and tax implications of exiting your LLC should not be underestimated. Depending on how the exit is structured, you might be subject to capital gains tax on the sale of the business. Planning ahead with a tax professional can help you minimize these liabilities by adjusting the timing of the sale or structuring it in a way that allows for more favorable tax treatment. Legally, the process might involve dissolving the LLC or transferring membership interests, each requiring specific steps and filings with your state and the IRS to ensure everything is buttoned up correctly.

Navigating the exit of your LLC involves a complex interplay of strategic planning, financial savvy, and legal knowledge. But more than that, it requires a deep understanding of what you want from the exit and what's best for the business you've built. Whether you're passing the torch to a successor or closing the doors for good, the goal is to honor the legacy of your LLC while paving the way for future successes, either for the business under new ownership or for yourself as you venture into new beginnings.

7.5 SUCCESSION PLANNING: PREPARING YOUR LLC FOR THE FUTURE

It's somewhat surreal. One day, you're sketching out business ideas on a napkin; the next, you're pondering who will carry on your legacy. That's the beauty and, admittedly, the bittersweet part of building something that matters. Succession planning isn't merely a strategy for transitioning; it's about ensuring the heartbeat of your LLC continues to thump strong, even if you decide to hang up your entrepreneurial hat or fate decides for you. Think of it as scripting the next episodes of your favorite series—you want the essence to live on, even if the original cast bows out.

The importance of having a solid succession plan in place can't be stressed enough. It's like putting on a seatbelt; you don't do it because you expect to crash but because it's essential to safeguard against the unexpected. Whether it's due to retirement, disability, or more somber reasons, the continuity and stability of your LLC hinge significantly on how well-prepared you are for handing over the reins. Without a clear plan, your business could face disruptions or dissolution, leaving your employees, customers, and even your legacy in limbo.

Identifying potential successors is akin to casting actors for those crucial next episodes. The fit must be just right whether you're considering family members, key employees, or even an external candidate. This isn't just about finding someone with the right skills; it's about aligning with someone who shares the vision and passion for your business's future. Start by evaluating the leadership qualities, commitment, and understanding of your business operations among your potential successors. It's a mix of gut feeling and hard evidence—like choosing a lead singer for your band; they must hit the right notes emotionally and professionally.

The real work begins once you've got your eyes set on a potential successor. Preparing them isn't an overnight task.

Think of it as a mentorship program where you're gradually transferring your knowledge and responsibilities. This could involve shadowing you in meetings, taking the lead on projects, or making decisions under your guidance. It's about giving them the wheels gradually until they're ready to drive. Ensuring a smooth transition means embedding them into the fabric of your business's culture and operations so that when the time comes, the shift feels natural to your team, stakeholders, and even your clientele.

Legal Documentation

As much as succession is about personal relationships and mentorship, it's equally a legal dance. Ensuring all the i's are dotted, and the t's are crossed involves formalizing your plans in legal documents. This might include amendments to your LLC's operating agreement to reflect new ownership structures or drafting buy-sell agreements that outline how ownership interests are sold or transferred. These documents act like the script of your succession plan, detailing every scene meticulously to avoid any improvisation that could lead to disputes or confusion.

Communicating the Plan

Finally, rolling out the red carpet for your succession plan means communicating it effectively to all relevant parties. It's like unveiling a new product; you want to generate buy-in and excitement. Start with your internal team; they are the backbone of your LLC and need to feel secure and informed about the future. Extend this communication to your key stakeholders—investors, suppliers, and long-term clients;

they should hear about the changes from you, not through the grapevine. Transparency here is paramount; it reassures everyone involved that the business they trust and rely on is in good hands.

Navigating succession planning is a profound journey. It's about reflecting on your business's past, securing its present, and carefully crafting its future. By recognizing the importance of succession planning, identifying and preparing the proper successor, ensuring the legal framework is solid, and communicating openly with all stakeholders, you're not just planning for an exit but setting the stage for enduring success. This thoughtful approach ensures that the legacy of your LLC, much like a well-loved novel, continues to inspire and thrive, chapter after chapter.

As we close this chapter on navigating complex LLC landscapes, from resolving disputes to planning for succession, it's clear that the journey of managing an LLC is both challenging and rewarding. Each section has woven a tapestry of strategies and insights, equipping you with the knowledge to handle whatever comes your way. Looking ahead, we focus on enhancing your LLC with technology, where we'll explore how modern tools can streamline operations, boost efficiency, and keep your business at the cutting edge. Let's step forward, ready to embrace the innovations that await.

ENHANCING YOUR LLC WITH TECHNOLOGY

Imagine your LLC as a high-performance sports car. Now, every sports car needs a skilled driver, sure, but they also require a top-notch dashboard equipped with the latest tech to monitor everything from speed to fuel efficiency. Similarly, managing your LLC at top efficiency isn't just about your entrepreneurial skills; it also hinges on leveraging the right management software. This suite of tools acts as your business's dashboard, helping you navigate through the complexities of modern business landscapes with greater precision and ease.

8.1 ESSENTIAL SOFTWARE TOOLS FOR LLC MANAGEMENT

Overview of Management Software

In the dynamic arena of LLC management, having robust software tools isn't just an advantage; it's a necessity. These tools range widely, covering everything from accounting and CRM to project management. Each type of software serves a unique function:

- **Accounting software** keeps track of your finances, processes invoices, and prepares you for tax time without a hitch.
- **CRM systems** manage your interactions with current and potential customers, store their information, and help tailor marketing strategies to enhance customer relationships.
- **Project management tools** help plan, organize, and manage resource tools and develop resource estimates.

Think of these software solutions as members of a pit crew, each expertly tuning a different part of your racing car, ensuring it runs smoothly and efficiently, ready to take on the competitive race of business.

Benefits of Integrated Software Systems

Now, while each software tool is powerful, its real magic lies in integration. Integrated software systems speak to each other, ensuring that data flows seamlessly from one application to another. This integration provides a holistic view of your business operations, akin to having a 360-degree camera on your car, giving you a complete view that enhances your decision-making and operational efficiency.

For instance, when your CRM system is integrated with your accounting software, data about customer purchases can automatically update the financial records, providing real-time insights into sales trends and customer behaviors without manual data entry. This reduces errors and frees up your time to focus on strategic decision-making rather than getting bogged down by administrative tasks.

Choosing the Right Software

Selecting the right software for your LLC can feel like navigating a tech expo—overwhelming due to the sheer number of options available. Here are some criteria to help you make an informed choice:

- **Scalability:** Can the software grow with your business? Like a car with adjustable seats that accommodate both short and long rides, your chosen software should be able to handle your business's growth, from more users to more complex processes.
- **User-friendliness:** Is the software easy to use or does it require extensive training? Opt for solutions with intuitive interfaces—think of it as choosing a car with a user-friendly dashboard where everything is at your fingertips.
- **Cost-effectiveness:** Does the software provide value for money? Ensure the benefits justify the investment, similar to choosing a car with excellent mileage that promises long-term savings on fuel.

Implementation Tips

Implementing new software is not just about installation; it's about ensuring it integrates smoothly into your business processes and enhances operational efficiency. Here are some best practices:

- **Conduct training sessions for staff:** Just as you would take a few driving lessons before hitting the road in a new sports car, ensure your team is well-versed in using the latest software. This training should cover the basics of using the software and how it fits into your broader business processes.
- **Set up data backup systems:** In the digital world, data is as precious as a car in a heated race. Set up robust data backup systems to protect your business from data loss due to unforeseen circumstances, such as cyberattacks or system failures.
- **Monitor the software's effectiveness regularly:** After implementation, track how the software impacts your business operations. Is it making processes faster? Is it providing the insights you need? This ongoing evaluation is like a regular car maintenance check—it helps you ensure that your investment is continually paying off.

By enhancing your LLC with the right technology, particularly effective management software, you're not just keeping pace with the modern business world; you're setting the pace, ensuring your business runs more like a well-oiled, high-performance sports car, ready to take the lead in the race to success.

8.2 USING SOCIAL MEDIA TO BOOST YOUR LLC'S VISIBILITY

Imagine stepping into a bustling market square, where every stall is vibrant, each vendor vying for attention, and every shout and song is a bid to attract more foot traffic. Now, transpose this scene to the digital world—that's social media for your LLC. Platforms like Facebook, Instagram, LinkedIn, and X are the stalls; your posts are your pitch. Each comment, like, and share is akin to a customer nodding appreciatively at your products. This bustling digital marketplace is where brands are built and customer relationships are cemented.

Let's start with a quick tour of the main streets in our digital marketplace. With its vast user base, Facebook acts like the main square—everyone is here, from your teenage niece to your grandma. It's ideal for building community around your brand, sharing updates, and engaging with customers through posts, live videos, and more. Instagram, on the other hand, is like a trendy art district. It's all about visuals—photos, short videos, and stories that capture the essence of your brand at a glance. Then there's LinkedIn, the business district perfect for networking and connecting with other professionals, sharing industry insights, and recruiting talent. And X? It's the bustling café down the street where news breaks fast, opinions are aired in real-time, and businesses can engage directly and swiftly with followers.

Crafting a social media strategy that aligns with your LLC's marketing goals is like drawing a market map before you set up your stall. You need to know what you're selling, who will most likely buy it, and the best way to catch their eye. Start by defining your target audience. Are they young professionals? Busy moms? Tech enthusiasts? Understanding who they are dictates where you should focus your efforts and what content will engage them. Your brand identity should shine through this content, whether it's the professionalism in your LinkedIn articles or the creativity in your Instagram posts.

Now, onto the art of content creation and scheduling. Think of this as planning your market days and specials. Consistency is key—regular posts keep your stall lively and engaging. Use scheduling tools to program your posts to coincide with when your audience is most active online. This ensures your content doesn't get lost in the noise. Sunday evenings might be great for a relaxed read on LinkedIn, while quick, catchy tweets might perform better during the weekday morning rush. Each piece of content should serve a purpose: to inform, entertain, or sell. A mix of formats can keep things interesting—photos, videos, infographics, or simple text posts. Remember, engagement is a two-way street; respond to comments, ask questions, and participate in conversations to build a community around your brand.

Leveraging paid advertising on these platforms can amplify your reach substantially, like paying for a prime spot in the market. Social media ads allow for precise targeting—demographics, interests, behaviors, and more—so your content reaches those most likely to engage with your brand. Ad budgeting depends on your marketing goals and the competition in your niche. Start small, test different ads, and measure their performance. How many people are clicking through to your website? Are your ads leading to sales or sign-ups? Adjust your strategy based on these metrics to ensure you're getting the best return on your investment.

Incorporating social media effectively into your LLC's marketing strategy transforms it from a mere presence in the digital marketplace to a dynamic participant that attracts, engages, and retains customers. It's about being visible, vocal, and valuable. As you navigate through this bustling market, remember that each post you make, ad you run, and interaction you have builds your brand's story. In this vibrant, ever-changing arena of social media, your ability to adapt and engage directly correlates with your LLC's ability to thrive. Keep your content fresh, your interactions genuine, and your strategy flexible, and watch as your digital stall draws a crowd.

8.3 E-COMMERCE STRATEGIES FOR LLCS

Stepping into the realm of e-commerce can be likened to opening a brand-new store, but in the digital neighborhood, foot traffic is replaced by web traffic, and shop windows are now vibrant website pages. Let's start with the first brick in your online storefront: setting up an e-commerce platform. Selecting the right platform is similar to choosing the location for your physical store; it needs to be accessible, reliable, and supportive of your business's unique needs. Platforms like Shopify, WooCommerce, and Magento offer varied features that cater to different sizes and types of companies. It's not just about picking the one with the most bells and whistles; it's about finding a platform that aligns with your operational style and business goals. Once chosen, the design of your website should prioritize user-friendliness. Imagine your customers navigating your store with a blindfold—everything should be so intuitive that they can still find what they need even without seeing. This means clear categories, a simple checkout process, and minimal clutter. Integrating payment processing systems is next, and it's crucial for making the payment process as smooth as pouring a glass of wine. Secure, versatile payment solutions that handle multiple payment methods, from credit cards to digital wallets, can significantly enhance the customer experience, making it as pleasant as a walk in the park.

Now, with your digital storefront set up, the focus shifts to optimizing online sales. This stage is about making your products irresistible and easy to find. Begin with your product descriptions; these are more than just factual statements about your items. They should tell a compelling story, highlighting the benefits and sparking imagination. Think of them as your sales pitch; every word should paint a picture that places the product right into the customers' lives, showcasing how it solves a problem or enhances their experience. High-quality images are equally crucial; they act as the dressing on your store window, attracting and engaging customers. Each image should be clear, professionally shot, and able to convey the quality and details of the product as if the customers were examining it with a magnifying glass. Implementing SEO (search engine optimization) best practices can amplify your visibility as much as a well-placed billboard on a busy highway. Keywords, meta descriptions, and alt texts aren't just buzzwords; they are your best allies in making your site more visible to search engines and helping guide more potential customers to your digital doorstep.

Enhancing the customer experience online is about ensuring every interaction with your e-commerce site is as smooth and enjoyable as sipping a fine wine. This starts with the website's performance; a slow-loading page can turn away customers faster than a closed sign on your front door. Ensuring your site is optimized for speed, with compressed images and streamlined code, can keep your digital doors swinging open. Mobile compatibility is another critical aspect. With more people browsing and shopping on smartphones, your e-commerce site needs to perform flawlessly on these devices, adapting to different screen sizes and touch interfaces as smoothly as a chameleon changes its colors. Exceptional customer service completes this trilogy of user experience. It's about being there for your customers whenever they need you, whether through a quick response to an email, a helpful live chat session, or a comprehensive FAQ section. Each positive interaction is like a brick in the foundation of customer trust and loyalty.

Lastly, the magic of e-commerce unfolds when you start digging into the analytics. Tools like Google Analytics act like high-powered microscopes, zooming into your business data and providing insights that are as valuable as finding a map in a treasure hunt. Understanding where your visitors come from, which products they linger on, and where in the buying process they decide to leave are all crucial data points. These insights allow you to make informed decisions, tailor your marketing strategies, and tweak your site to meet your customers' needs better. It's about turning raw data into actionable wisdom, ensuring every tweak and twist in your strategy is guided by fundamental user interactions, and drawing a clear path toward business growth and customer satisfaction.

By weaving together these strategies—from setting up the right e-commerce platform and optimizing product listings to enhancing the user experience and diving deep into analytics—you can turn your LLC's e-commerce venture from just another online store into a thriving digital marketplace. It's about crafting an environment where customers don't just visit but stay, shop, and return, driven by a seamless blend of technology, strategy, and genuine customer-centricity.

8.4 CYBERSECURITY MEASURES FOR PROTECTING YOUR LLC ONLINE

Imagine you've just installed the most sophisticated lock on your front door to keep your home safe and sound. Now, think of cybersecurity in the same way, but instead of just one door, you have a whole network of doors and windows in the form of your LLC's digital presence. It's crucial to understand that while offering boundless opportunities, the digital world also comes with its share of ne'er-do-wells—cyber threats that can compromise your business's integrity and security. Common threats like malware, which can infiltrate and disrupt your systems, phishing scams that trick you into giving away sensitive information, and ransomware, which is akin to a digital hostage situation where your data is locked until you pay a ransom, are just a few of the dangers lurking in the digital shadows.

The potential impact of these threats on an LLC can range from mild inconvenience to catastrophic data loss that could devastate your business operations. For instance, malware can corrupt your files and systems, leading to significant downtime as you scramble to recover data and restore systems. Phishing attacks can lead to unauthorized access to sensitive business information, damaging your reputation and potentially leading to financial losses. Ransomware can completely halt your business operations, locking you out of your data and systems until a hefty ransom is paid. Each of these scenarios can be devastating, but the good news is that they can be mitigated with the proper cybersecurity measures.

Implementing strong cybersecurity practices is like setting up a comprehensive security system for your digital house. Start with the basics: strong passwords. It might seem trivial, but robust passwords act like sturdy locks on every entry point. They should be complex, unique for each system, and changed regularly. Think of them as constantly evolving safeguards that keep intruders guessing. Next, enable two-factor authentication (2FA) wherever possible. This adds an additional layer of security, ensuring that the chances of unauthorized access are minimized even if a password is compromised. It's like having a double-lock feature on your doors.

Regularly updating software is another critical step. Software developers regularly release updates that add new features and fix security vulnerabilities. Keeping your software up to date ensures these vulnerabilities are patched before cybercriminals can exploit them. It's like reinforcing your windows before a storm; it might be sunny now, but you'll be glad for the protection when the weather turns.

Training your employees on cybersecurity awareness is equally crucial. After all, the most sophisticated security systems can be undone by human error. Conduct regular training sessions to educate your team on the importance of cybersecurity, the common threats, and best practices for safe online behavior. Teach them to recognize the signs of phishing emails, the importance of using secure networks, and the protocols to follow when they suspect a security breach. This training turns your employees from potential security vulnerabilities into informed defenders of your digital domain.

Lastly, developing a cybersecurity incident response plan is imperative. Despite your best efforts, breaches can happen, and having a plan in place ensures you can respond effectively and efficiently. This plan should outline the steps to take immediately after discovering a breach, including how to contain the breach to prevent further damage, whom to notify about the incident—from stakeholders to legal authorities—and how to recover any lost data. It should also include post-incident analysis to determine how the breach occurred and measures to prevent future incidents. This plan isn't just a procedural document; it's a blueprint for action during digital emergencies, ensuring that your LLC can withstand and recover from cyber threats with resilience.

By understanding the cyber threats specific to small businesses, implementing robust security measures, training your team, and preparing a solid response plan, you can protect your LLC from the vast majority of digital dangers. This proactive approach not only safeguards your business data but also preserves the trust and confidence of your clients, reinforcing your reputation as a secure and reliable business. In the digital age, where threats evolve rapidly, staying vigilant and prepared is your best strategy for keeping your digital doors locked and your business safe.

8.5 INCORPORATING AI AND AUTOMATION IN YOUR BUSINESS PROCESSES

When we discuss integrating AI and automation into your business, imagine handing over tedious, time-consuming tasks to a team of ultra-efficient robots. These aren't the clunky machines from old sci-fi movies; these are sophisticated, intelligent systems designed to streamline your operations and free you up to focus on what really matters— growing your business and enhancing customer relationships.

AI and automation are transforming the business landscape, making operations smoother and more efficient. For instance, AI can handle data analysis, predict market trends, and even manage customer service interactions without breaking a sweat. Automation takes over repetitive tasks like scheduling, data entry, and fundamental customer interactions, ensuring these tasks are completed faster and with fewer errors than ever before.

Let's explore how AI tools can revolutionize customer interactions, particularly in customer service. Chatbots and virtual assistants powered by AI can be your frontliners when handling customer inquiries. They're available 24/7, don't need coffee breaks, and never tire. Picture this: A customer visits your website at midnight, looking for information about your product. Instead of waiting until morning to get a response from a human, a chatbot greets them instantly, answers their queries, and even helps them make a purchase decision. This level of responsiveness can significantly enhance customer satisfaction and turn casual browsers into loyal customers.

Moreover, automation in operations can be a game-changer. Consider the time-intensive process of invoicing or payroll management. Automation tools can handle these tasks effortlessly, reducing the risk of human error and ensuring things like payments and account management are handled with precision. This helps maintain a healthy cash flow and keeps your employees and vendors happy with timely payouts.

However, implementing AI and automation requires careful planning. It's about seamlessly choosing and integrating the right tools into your existing processes. This might involve some trial and error and adjustment as your team gets used to the new systems. Regularly monitoring these AI and automation systems is crucial to ensure they are operational and optimal. This involves periodically checking their performance, analyzing how they impact your productivity, and making adjustments as necessary. Think of it as routine maintenance for a high-performance engine—you must keep tuning it to get the best out of it.

Monitoring and Optimizing AI Systems

You need to closely monitor these systems to make AI and automation work for your LLC. It's not enough to set them up and forget them; you must monitor their performance and continually optimize them. This might sound daunting, but it can be manageable with the right tools and approaches.

One effective strategy is to use analytics to track the performance of your AI tools. Most AI systems have built-in analytics features; you can integrate them with third-party analytics tools. These tools can provide insights into how well the AI handles tasks, where it excels, and where it may fall short. For example, suppose you're using AI for customer chat support. In that case, analytics can show you response times, customer satisfaction ratings, and conversion rates from interactions handled by AI versus those handled by humans.

Based on these insights, you can make informed decisions about how to improve your AI systems. The chatbot may need better training to handle certain types of inquiries, or automation in inventory management can be tweaked to predict better stock levels based on sales trends. It's all about refining these tools so they work more effectively for your business.

Incorporating AI and automation into your LLC can feel like moving into a futuristic world where machines handle the mundane, leaving you free to focus on innovation and growth. By choosing the right tools, integrating them thoughtfully into your business processes, and continually monitoring and optimizing their performance, you can harness the full power of AI and automation to transform your business operations. This boosts efficiency and accuracy and gives you a competitive edge in today's fast-paced business environment.

As we wrap up this exploration of AI and automation, remember that these technologies are not just about cutting costs or increasing efficiency—they are about enhancing the capabilities of your LLC and opening up new opportunities for growth and innovation. By embracing AI and automation, you're setting your business up for future success, ready to meet the challenges of tomorrow with the best that technology has to offer.

The next chapter will focus on another crucial aspect of modern business operations—sustainability practices. We'll explore how integrating sustainable practices can help protect the environment and build a more substantial, resilient business.

CASE STUDIES AND REAL-WORLD APPLICATIONS

Imagine entering a room filled with entrepreneurs, each with a story blending minor missteps and significant triumphs. This chapter is like that room. Here, you'll get an insider's view of how various LLCs navigated through choppy waters to find their rhythm and thrive. These narratives are not just stories; they are blueprints laden with practical wisdom and strategic insights that can guide you as you carve out your path in the business world. Let's pull up a chair and learn from those who've walked this path before us.

9.1 CASE STUDY: OVERCOMING EARLY CHALLENGES IN AN LLC

Starting an LLC can often feel like assembling a massive puzzle where half the pieces are hidden and the rest don't fit. The early days are crucial and frequently fraught with challenges that can make or break the future of a business. Let's delve into a case study of EcoEssentials LLC, a startup that faced its fair share of hurdles but emerged victorious by employing strategic maneuvers and innovative thinking.

Identifying Initial Obstacles

EcoEssentials LLC began with a grand vision: revolutionizing the eco-friendly products market. However, the journey kicked off with a bumpy start. Cash flow management was their first monster under the bed—the influx of expenses before the cash flow stabilized led to sleepless nights for the founders. Client acquisition followed close behind. Convincing consumers to switch to a new, eco-conscious brand was more challenging than convincing a toddler that broccoli is candy. Regulatory compliance was the maze they hadn't anticipated. Navigating through certifications and standards necessary for their products proved more complex than they had expected.

Strategies Employed

The path to stabilization required agility and inventive strategies. EcoEssentials LLC didn't shy away from thinking outside the box. They embarked on a dual approach to tackle their cash flow issues. First, they initiated a pre-order system to gauge demand without overcommitting resources. Second, they adopted a just-in-time inventory system to keep the storage costs at bay. The company leveraged social media for client acquisition to launch targeted awareness campaigns that educated potential customers on the benefits of switching to eco-friendly products. They showcased customer testimonials and third-party certifications to build trust and credibility.

Strategic partnerships played a pivotal role. By collaborating with established names in the eco-space, EcoEssentials LLC tapped into existing customer bases and gained valuable market insights. These partnerships also aided in smoothing out the regulatory hurdles, as they could lean on the experience and resources of their partners.

Turning Points

The decision to shift their marketing strategy toward storytelling was a significant turning point. Instead of merely selling products, EcoEssentials LLC began sharing stories about how each product benefited the user and the planet. This emotional and personal touch resonated with their audience, turning casual browsers into loyal customers and vocal advocates.

Financial planning was another critical area that needed a revamp. The founders started with a basic understanding of finances but soon realized the complexity of managing business finances. They invested in a financial planning tool that offered insights into cash flow trends, expense categorization, and economic forecasting. This tool became their financial compass, guiding them through the financial fog with clarity.

Lesson Sharing

From EcoEssentials LLC's journey, several lessons can be drawn. First, understanding and managing cash flow is crucial. Tools and strategies that provide real-time insights into your finances can be game-changers. Second, authenticity and education are essential for client acquisition. People connect with stories and purposes, not just products. Lastly, don't underestimate the power of strategic partnerships. They can provide shortcuts through learning curves and open doors you didn't even know existed.

In this ever-evolving business landscape, the challenges you face today might pave the way for your triumphs tomorrow. Each obstacle is an opportunity to learn, adapt, and grow. Like EcoEssentials LLC, your LLC can turn early challenges into stepping stones toward lasting success. Remember, it's about avoiding pitfalls and building a bridge that leads to your goals. Keep these lessons close as you navigate your path; you may find that the most significant challenges often lead to the most rewarding successes.

9.2 CASE STUDY: INNOVATIVE TAX HANDLING IN A TECH LLC

Imagine a tech LLC, let's call it Innovatech Solutions, that started in a small garage with big dreams and a handful of resourceful tech enthusiasts. As Innovatech grew from a local startup to a buzzing hive of activity with clients across the globe, the complexity of their tax responsibilities grew too. The company wrestled with a Gordian knot of tax scenarios due to its rapid expansion, diverse revenue streams, and cross-border transactions. It's like suddenly realizing you're in a chess game where every move affects your survival, and you must think five moves ahead.

Innovatech's leadership recognized early on that conventional tax-handling methods wouldn't cut it. They needed strategies as innovative as the technologies they developed.

One of the first avenues they explored was taking full advantage of research and development (R&D) tax credits. This isn't just about getting a pat on the back for inventing cool stuff; it's a substantial financial boon that can slash tax liabilities for companies investing in new technology and innovation. Innovatech meticulously documented its development processes, ensuring every qualifying activity was recorded. This wasn't just about keeping the taxman happy but about reclaiming funds to be reinvested into pushing the tech envelope even further.

But why stop at local benefits when you can go global? Innovatech expanded its operations into new markets, where the plot thickens—they leveraged international tax treaties. These treaties can be lifesavers, preventing double taxation of the same income in two countries. It's like having diplomatic immunity in the realm of global commerce. Innovatech worked with tax professionals to navigate this complex web of agreements, ensuring they optimized their tax positions without stepping on legal landmines.

Then came a game-changer—strategic entity structuring. Innovatech restructured its business entities based on geographic and operational needs, akin to rearranging the pieces on your chessboard to maximize defense and attack. Establishing subsidiaries in different countries reduced the effective tax rate and shielded the parent company from potential financial risks. This strategic move isn't just about saving a few bucks; it's about ensuring longevity and stability in the volatile world of tech.

The impact? It was like watching a phoenix rise. The savings from these tax strategies significantly bolstered Innovatech's financial health. Instead, funds that would have filled tax coffers were funneled into R&D and hiring top-tier talent. They could afford to take more significant risks and innovate faster, knowing their tax strategies provided a safety net below their fiscal high-wire act.

For fellow tech LLC owners, this tale isn't just a bedtime story; it's a treasure map. Here are some nuggets of wisdom to pocket: First, don't view taxes as a mere obligation; see them as a puzzle that, when solved, can liberate resources for your business. Engage with tax professionals who need to see numbers and understand your industry's nuances. Document meticulously, as if you're crafting a novel about your company's journey, ensuring every significant action is recorded for potential tax credits. And finally, think globally, even if you're operating locally. Tax treaties and strategic entity structures might seem overkill when small, but they'll be your anchors in the whirlwind of growth.

Navigating the tax labyrinth with agility and foresight can transform tax from a dreaded drain on your resources into a strategic tool that propels your business forward. Innovatech Solutions stands as a testament to what's possible when you approach tax with as much innovation as you do your product development—turning a potential headache into a strategic victory.

9.3 CASE STUDY: INFUSING A FAMILY-OWNED LLC

Infusing a family-owned LLC with adequate asset protection strategies resembles weaving a sturdy safety net under a trapeze act. It's about ensuring that the family's personal and business assets are safeguarded against the unexpected flips and turns of the business world. Let's dive into the story of Heritage Crafters LLC, a family-owned business specializing in artisan furniture. It was at a crossroads where business interests and family dynamics intertwined.

Asset Protection Needs

For Heritage Crafters LLC, the blend of family and business meant that their asset protection strategies needed to be particularly robust. The family's personal assets, such as their homes and savings, were initially tangled up with the business assets, which included the workshop, tools, and inventory. This intermingling posed a significant risk; a lawsuit against the business could wipe out the business assets and the family's wealth. Moreover, the family's emotional ties added complexity to decision-making processes, making it crucial to delineate clear boundaries between personal and business finances to prevent internal conflicts.

Structural Decisions Made

Recognizing these challenges, the family implemented several strategic legal structures and agreements to fortify their asset protection. First, they established a trust to shield their personal assets. This move effectively separated their personal wealth from the business assets, ensuring that the family's financial health would remain intact regardless of the business's legal entanglements. Next, they restructured Heritage Crafters LLC into distinct operational entities. Doing so confined any potential liabilities to the entity directly involved, preventing a domino effect that could impact the entire business structure.

Additionally, the family drafted a clear and comprehensive family succession plan. This document was not just a legal formality but a crucial step in maintaining harmony and ensuring a smooth leadership and ownership transition. It detailed the roles and responsibilities of each family member, the process for onboarding future generations, and the conditions under which ownership would transfer. This planning helped mitigate any ambiguity that could lead to disputes, ensuring that the business and family relationships could thrive.

Outcome and Benefits

The outcomes of these strategic decisions were profoundly positive. By safeguarding their personal assets through a trust, the family enjoyed peace of mind, knowing their finances were secure from business liabilities. The operational restructuring into distinct entities proved wise during a turbulent economic phase when one part of the business faced a lawsuit. Due to the separation, the lawsuit affected only the entity involved, leaving the other aspects of the company and the family's personal assets untouched.

Furthermore, the clear family succession plan ensured that leadership transitions were smooth and free from the power struggles that often plague family businesses. This forward-thinking approach preserved family wealth and minimized liability risks, providing the company's long-term viability.

Best Practices

From the experience of Heritage Crafters LLC, several best practices emerge for other family-owned LLCs navigating the complex terrain of asset protection. First, the separation of personal and business assets is paramount. Consider establishing trusts or legal entities to protect individual wealth from business liabilities. Secondly, transparency and clear communication are crucial, especially when multiple family members are involved. Regular family meetings to discuss business operations, challenges, and strategies can foster unity and prevent misunderstandings.

Lastly, prepare for the future with a comprehensive family succession plan. Such planning secures a smooth transition and reinforces the business's stability and the family's commitment to each other and the enterprise. In essence, weaving a tight safety net of legal and financial protections not only safeguards assets but fortifies the family bonds, ensuring that the business can continue flourishing without risking the family's harmony and wealth.

As we explore these strategies and their impacts, remember that every family and business situation is unique. The key is to adapt these principles to fit your specific circumstances, ensuring that your family-owned LLC can withstand the storms of the business world while keeping the family foundation solid and secure.

9.4 CASE STUDY: SCALING AN LLC FROM LOCAL TO GLOBAL

Scaling a business from a cozy local market to the bustling global stage is like transitioning from performing in your hometown's community theater to headlining concerts across continents. It's thrilling, yes, but it's also packed with nuances that can make or break your grand debut on the world stage. Let's unwrap the story of GlobeTech LLC, a tech startup that began its journey in a small Midwestern town and rose to claim a global footprint, offering lessons on scalability that are as golden as any high-stakes venture could hope for.

Growth Milestones

GlobeTech LLC started as a modest software development firm catering to local businesses. Their first significant growth milestone was developing a unique project management tool that gained traction beyond their immediate geographic area. This unexpected popularity was their cue to think bigger. The subsequent milestones were carefully plotted points on their growth chart, from expanding their service offerings to AI-driven analytics solutions to opening their first overseas office in London. Each milestone was a marker of growth and a testament to their adaptability and ambition. It's like watching a series where each episode builds on the last, widening the storyline and deepening the plot.

Strategies for International Expansion

GlobeTech's international expansion was not a spur-of-the-moment decision but a series of strategic moves. They started with exhaustive market research to identify which regions held the most promise for their technology solutions. Understanding local market dynamics, consumer behavior, and competitive landscapes was crucial. It's similar to learning the rules of the road when driving in a new country—you don't just take the wheel and hope for the best.

Partnering with local firms was another strategic masterstroke. GlobeTech formed alliances with companies in target regions to gain insights into local business practices and consumer expectations. These partnerships were bridges into new territories, helping to navigate the cultural and regulatory nuances that could easily be roadblocks. They adapted their products to meet local needs, a process akin to tweaking a recipe to cater to local tastes—keeping the core but adjusting the flavors to suit the palate.

Challenges and Solutions

However, GlobeTech's road to global presence was not without its bumps. One of the first challenges was logistical complexities. Managing supply chains and operations across different time zones was as daunting as conducting an orchestra where every musician is in a different country. They implemented a 24-hour operational model, divided betweeen their offices in different time zones, ensuring that someone was always steering the ship, whether at noon or midnight.

Regulatory compliance was another significant hurdle. Each country presented a new set of legal frameworks with which they had to comply. GlobeTech tackled this by hiring local legal experts in each region, ensuring they played by the book, no matter where they set up shop. Marketing strategies also had to be overhauled. What worked in the U.S. did not necessarily charm audiences in Asia or Europe. They crafted localized marketing campaigns that resonated with regional narratives and values, much like a playwright adapts dialogues to suit the local dialect without losing the script's essence.

Scalability Lessons

The scalability saga of GlobeTech LLC offers invaluable lessons for other LLCs eyeing the global stage. Flexibility and local engagement emerged as the cornerstones of successful scaling. Adapting to diverse market needs and effectively integrating local insights into business strategies was pivotal. Moreover, the importance of building a reliable local team must be addressed. These people understand the market's pulse and can navigate the local business terrain more efficiently and effectively.

Scaling an LLC from local to global is an exhilarating adventure, marked by transformative growth and learning curves that are as steep as they are rewarding. For those looking to expand their horizons, remember that the world is vast and the opportunities are limitless. With the right strategies, a deep understanding of local markets, and an adaptable approach, your LLC can enter and command the global stage.

9.5 LESSONS LEARNED FROM FAILED LLCS AND HOW TO AVOID SIMILAR MISTAKES

Turning the spotlight on failed LLCs might feel like we're focusing on doom and gloom but think of it as learning to dance in the rain rather than waiting for the storm to pass. It's about gathering wisdom from missteps and misfortunes that others have experienced so that your LLC can waltz through challenges with grace and agility. Let's dissect some common pitfalls that have tripped up numerous ventures, explore the warning signs that often go unnoticed, and arm you with strategies to survive and thrive in the competitive business landscape.

Common Pitfalls

First, let's talk about poor financial management, akin to navigating a ship with no compass or map. Imagine setting sail on the high seas without knowing how to manage your provisions or plot your course. Similarly, LLCs that mismanage their finances might be adrift in turbulent waters. Whether overspending on nonessential services or underestimating the necessity of a solid cash reserve, financial mismanagement can quickly capsize a business.

Another treacherous pitfall is inadequate legal preparations. It's like building a house with no foundation. It might stand for a while, especially when the weather's fair, but it won't withstand the first storm. Many LLCs skimp on legal groundwork, either from a desire to cut costs or simple oversight. This lack of legal fortification can lead to severe consequences, from tax penalties to more dire legal disputes that could threaten the business's very existence.

Lastly, let's consider flawed business models. This issue resembles a playwright insisting on a script the audience doesn't connect with. No matter how great the production, the show will flop if the script is off. An LLC with a business model that doesn't resonate with its target market or fails to adapt to changing market dynamics is like that stubborn playwright. It's not just about having a product or service to sell; it's about understanding the market and continuously evolving to meet its needs and desires.

Warning Signs

Recognizing the early signs of trouble can help steer your LLC away from potential pitfalls. One such sign is declining sales, which can indicate a saturated market, an outdated product, or a pricing strategy that's not hitting the right note. It's time to reassess and pivot your strategy.

High employee turnover is another red flag. It's often a symptom of deeper issues, such as poor management, inadequate compensation, or a toxic company culture. Employees are the lifeblood of any business; a high turnover rate can disrupt operations and erode institutional knowledge, weakening the company from the inside.

Increasing debt is a particularly alarming sign and one that demands immediate attention. It could result from overexpansion, poor financial management, or simply needing to keep a close enough eye on the bottom line. Like water seeping into the hull of a ship, increasing debt can sink a business if not addressed promptly.

Preventive Measures

To avoid these pitfalls, regular business audits are crucial. Think of it as going to the doctor for a check-up, even when you feel healthy. These audits help identify issues before they become serious threats, ensuring your business stays on track and healthy.

Enhanced strategic planning is another essential preventive measure. This involves setting goals and regularly reviewing and adjusting those goals to align with the evolving market landscape. It's about being proactive rather than reactive, staying two steps ahead of potential challenges.

Seeking expert advice is always a wise strategy. Whether it's a financial advisor, a legal consultant, or an industry mentor, gaining insights from those with experience and expertise can provide you with a valuable perspective that might be missing from your current strategy. It's like having a seasoned navigator aboard your ship, helping you chart the safest and most efficient course.

Recovery Strategies

If your LLC does face setbacks, consider it a detour rather than a dead-end. Pivoting business strategies can breathe new life into your venture. This might mean overhauling your marketing strategy, rethinking your product line, or changing your business model. It's about being flexible and adaptable, willing to make tough decisions to save the ship.

Restructuring the business can also be a viable strategy for recovery. This might involve streamlining operations, focusing on more profitable product lines, or even downsizing to reduce overhead costs until the business can regain its footing.

Exploring exit options is another route. Sometimes, the best decision for the financial health of the business owners and stakeholders is to close down or sell the business. This isn't giving up; it's strategically choosing to preserve what can be saved and possibly prepare for a new venture with better prospects.

In wrapping up this exploration into the lessons learned from LLC failures, remember that each story holds critical insights that can fortify your business strategies. By understanding and avoiding common pitfalls, recognizing the warning signs, implementing preventive measures, and being prepared with recovery strategies, your LLC can navigate challenges and emerge stronger. Sometimes, the most profound lessons are learned not through success but through overcoming failures.

As we close this chapter, we pave the way into the subsequent exciting discussion on sustainability practices in business, where we will explore how integrating eco-friendly and sustainable methods can help save our planet and enhance your business's reputation and efficiency. Stay tuned, as this next chapter promises to enrich your entrepreneurial journey with green wisdom!

BEYOND THE BASICS: NEXT STEPS FOR YOUR THRIVING LLC

Imagine standing at the edge of a vast ocean, your LLC snugly in a boat beside you, ready to sail beyond the familiar horizon. Until now, you've navigated the tranquil waters of your local market, but the siren call of international shores is too alluring to ignore. Embarking on this expansive journey is not just about charting unknown territories—it's about discovering a world of possibilities that could elevate your LLC from a local favorite to a global icon. So, let's hoist the sails and set a course for international success, shall we?

10.1 EXPLORING INTERNATIONAL MARKETS WITH YOUR LLC

Assessing Market Viability

Before you can conquer new lands, you need to know the terrain. Assessing the viability of international markets is akin to being an explorer in the Age of Discovery, equipped with a modern GPS—market research. This crucial first step involves understanding each potential market's cultural nuances, economic stability, and consumer behavior. It's about asking questions like: Are the local consumers ready for your product? What local competitors will you face? How do economic conditions affect purchasing power?

To effectively gauge these factors, dive deep into market research methodologies ranging from analyzing market trends and consumer surveys to engaging with local consultants who breathe the local market air daily. Remember, each market has its own set of unwritten rules and preferences; what works back home may not resonate here. For example, while your eco-friendly packaging might be a hit in environmentally conscious regions, it might not sway consumers in areas where cost-effectiveness reigns supreme.

Navigating Legal and Regulatory Frameworks

If market viability is about knowing the waters, navigating legal and regulatory frameworks is about understanding the currents and undercurrents that can impact your voyage. Each country has its own business laws, import/export regulations, and tax treaties, which can either be stepping stones or stumbling blocks.

Think of this as assembling a puzzle where each piece represents a legal requirement or regulatory compliance. You must piece together these elements meticulously to avoid potential penalties or business interruptions. This might involve registering your business locally, understanding tax obligations, and adhering to local employment laws.

Engaging with legal experts in each country can be as crucial as having a local guide in a labyrinthine city. They can provide insights and navigate complex legal landscapes, ensuring your business complies with local laws and international agreements.

Building International Partnerships

No man—or business—is an island, especially when stepping into the global arena. Building solid local partnerships and strategic alliances can be your greatest asset. These partnerships can help you understand local market dynamics, distribute your products effectively, and navigate bureaucratic challenges more smoothly.

When selecting the right partners, think of it like choosing a dance partner for a waltz. You need someone who knows the steps, keeps time, and can glide with you seamlessly across the dance floor. This means looking for partners whose business objectives align with yours, who share your values, and who can enhance your business's reach and capabilities. Structuring these partnerships will require clear agreements that outline each party's roles, expectations, and contributions to avoid stepping on each other's toes.

Logistics and Supply Chain Management

Now, let's talk about the backbone of any international operation—logistics and supply chain management. Managing the flow of goods from your local warehouse to global markets is no less complex than orchestrating a symphony.

Each element, from production to delivery, must be timed perfectly and performed exactly as needed.

Developing efficient logistics involves several vital strategies. First, understand the import/export regulations affecting your shipping routes and costs. Second, choose reliable logistics partners to ensure your products travel safely and arrive on time. Third, consider the technology that can help track shipments and manage inventory effectively. Remember, the smoother your logistics, the quicker your products reach the market, and the faster you can generate revenue.

As you contemplate these expansive steps, remember that exploring international markets is not just about business growth—it's about embarking on an adventure that tests your limits, expands your horizons, and ultimately transforms your LLC into a global player. Ready your maps, set your compass, and let's sail into the vast, promising ocean of international business.

10.2 ADVANCED LEGAL CONSIDERATIONS FOR MATURE LLCS

As your LLC blooms and branches out beyond its roots, navigating the intricate dance of international business becomes more akin to choreographing a ballet than freestyling at a local club. You're playing in the big leagues now, which calls for a beefed-up legal game, especially when protecting the intellectual seeds you've sown—your intellectual property (IP). Imagine your IP as the golden eggs of your enterprise; in the global marketplace, it's not just about laying them but ensuring they're fortified against international poachers. Securing international patents and trademarks isn't just filling out some extra paperwork; it's about weaving a protective tapestry across multiple jurisdictions. Each country has its own set of rules and nuances for IP protection, which can feel like trying to solve a Rubik's cube blindfolded. But fear not; the effort to align these multicolored legal blocks ensures that your innovations and brand identity are safeguarded across borders, deterring infringements and setting a legal perimeter around your creative landscape.

Now, let's talk shop about the nitty-gritty of complex contract negotiations. If IP protection is about safeguarding your golden eggs, then mastering contract negotiations is about ensuring that these eggs can reach the market without getting scrambled. When dealing with international suppliers, clients, and partners, consider each contract a detailed recipe you're exchanging with a fellow chef. You wouldn't want them swapping your carefully selected organic ingredients for something less savory. Hence, embedding clauses that protect your interests and ensure compliance with international laws is crucial. It's about more than legalese: crafting a narrative within the contract that aligns with your business values and operational standards, ensuring every party is on the same page, or, in this case, a recipe card.

Risk management and liability reduction are where you put on your superhero cape because, let's face it, every business, no matter how well-run, faces its share of kryptonite. As your LLC grows, so do the stakes and potential risks. Implementing comprehensive risk management strategies isn't just about dodging legal bullets; it's about creating an armor that protects against them. This includes everything from choosing the right business insurance—think of it as your business's safety net—to fine-tuning your corporate structure, which can be as pivotal as a knight strategically moving on a chessboard. Indemnity clauses, for example, are not just legal jargon; they are your shield in the business battle, ensuring that liabilities are clearly defined and mitigated.

Lastly, let's talk legacy—no, not the kind you leave in a will but the kind that involves succession planning for your LLC. As you steer your enterprise into the future, thinking about who will take the wheel after you is not just prudent; it's essential for the continuity of your legacy. This isn't about handing over the keys to the kingdom on a whim. It's about a carefully orchestrated passing of the torch that ensures your business survives and thrives under new leadership. Legal considerations for transferring international operations involve complex maneuvers, akin to a relay race where the baton must be passed smoothly to avoid a fumble. It's about ensuring a seamless transition, adhering to international business laws, and aligning with the strategic vision you've set for your LLC.

Navigating these advanced legal terrains requires a blend of savvy, foresight, and, sometimes, a bit of legal acrobatics. But with the right strategies in place, your LLC can protect its assets and interests and pave the way for a legacy that crosses borders and generations. As you fortify your legal frameworks, remember that it's not just about guarding against risks; it's about creating a resilient foundation that allows your business to expand and excel in the global marketplace.

10.3 LONG-TERM FINANCIAL PLANNING AND INVESTMENT STRATEGIES FOR LLC OWNERS

Let's talk money but not just any money—the kind that ensures your later years are as vibrant and secure as your entrepreneurial spirit. Diversifying investments might sound like something from a Wall Street tycoon's handbook, but it's your financial safety net as an LLC owner. Think of it this way: Just as you wouldn't rely on a single client for all your income, you shouldn't rely on your business alone for your financial future. Diversification is about spreading your financial eggs across different baskets. Whether it's real estate, the stock market, bonds, or mutual funds, each type of investment has its own set of risks and rewards. Real estate can offer tangible assets and potential rental income, while stocks are about owning a piece of a company with the potential for dividends and appreciation. On the other hand, bonds are the more steady, reliable cousins, often providing fixed interest over time. By balancing these options, you can stabilize your income streams even when the market is as unpredictable as a plot twist in a mystery novel.

Now, onto a topic that might make even the most dauntless entrepreneurs sweat—retirement planning. Here's the scoop: Many entrepreneurs are so engrossed in their businesses that they forget to plan for the day they'll hang up their entrepreneurial hats. Since traditional employment benefits like a pension might not be in your cards, setting up a self-employed retirement plan is crucial. Options such as a solo 401(k) or a simplified employee pension plan (SEP) IRA allow you to save significantly more than traditional retirement accounts, and they come with tax advantages that can reduce your taxable income. It's like packing a parachute before jumping out of a plane—you want to be prepared before you take the leap into retirement.

Reinvesting in your business is much like watering a garden. It's not just about sustaining it; it's about helping it grow, blossom, and thrive. When profits start rolling in, treating yourself to a new car or a fancy vacation might be tempting. While that's not entirely off-limits, consider reinvesting a portion of those profits into your business. This could mean upgrading your technology, expanding your product line, or boosting your marketing efforts to reach new demographics. Think of it as planting the seeds for future harvests. However, this isn't about pouring money into the business mindlessly. It's about strategic allocation, ensuring that every dollar you reinvest is likely to generate a return, much like a skilled gardener knows precisely when and where to plant each seed.

Estate planning and asset transfer might bring to mind images of old tycoons in vast mansions, but it's about ensuring all the hard work you've put into your business pays off—not just for you but for your heirs or successors. This involves setting up legal structures, such as trusts or wills, to ensure a smooth transfer of your business and personal assets when the time comes. It's about protecting your legacy from taxes and legal complications during asset transfer. Think of it as crafting a detailed instruction manual for your LLC that others can follow, ensuring that your business continues to operate smoothly, even when you're not at the helm.

Navigating these financial strategies isn't just about bolstering your business—it's about securing a prosperous and stable future for yourself and your loved ones. By diversifying your investments, planning for retirement, strategically reinvesting in your business, and setting up a thorough estate plan, you are not just surviving in the business world but setting the stage for enduring success.

As we wrap up this chapter, remember that the essence of financial planning and investment for an LLC owner isn't just in accumulating wealth—it's in wisely managing and safeguarding that wealth through every phase of your business and personal life. This solid financial foundation not only supports your current entrepreneurial endeavors but also paves the way for future generations or endeavors, ensuring that the legacy of your hard work extends far beyond your years at the helm.

SHARE YOUR EXPERIENCE!

Your experience is valuable, so no matter where you are on your LLC journey, take a moment to share it – it could make all the difference to someone else.

Simply by sharing your honest opinion of this book and a little about your experience, you'll not only show new readers where they can find this guidance; you'll give them more knowledge and experience that they can draw on to inform their own journey.

Thank you so much for your support. I wish you the very best of luck with your business.

Click here to leave your review on Amazon.
https://a.co/d/98i3KrU

CONCLUSION

Well, here we are at the end of our LLC adventure together, and what a journey it's been! From the initial steps of forming your LLC to navigating the complex waters of international expansion, this book has aimed to strip away the complexities and lay a clear path for you. Remember, the goal was never to inform but to empower you, to turn what might seem like a business maze into a straightforward walk in the park.

We've covered a lot, haven't we? From the nuts and bolts of setting up your LLC with its flexibility and robust liability protection to the savvy maneuvers of tax planning and asset protection, each piece of advice was designed to protect and propel your business forward, creating a solid foundation that supports growth and innovation.

But as we've seen, laying the foundation is just the beginning. The true art of LLC ownership is in the continuous dance of learning and adapting. Laws change, markets shift, and technology evolves. Staying informed and agile, ready to tweak strategies and embrace new tools, is not just helpful—it's essential.

I urge you to take these strategies—from leveraging powerful software to protect your digital assets to exploring new markets with a keen eye on cultural nuances—and put them into practice. Let the real-world case studies we explored serve as cautionary tales and inspirational roadmaps. Whether it's the tech startup that scaled globally or the family business that secured its legacy, these stories are nuggets of wisdom for practical application.

And let's remember the role of technology in this modern era. Embracing it is more than an option; staying competitive and efficient is necessary. Technology is the backbone of a thriving LLC, from automating your payroll to securing your data and scaling your marketing efforts.

However, while this book is a comprehensive guide, some scenarios require tailored advice. Feel free to seek legal or financial experts when encountering complex issues. It's not just about solving problems—it's about seizing opportunities to enhance your business's potential.

So, what's next for you? If you're on the brink of launching your LLC, it's time to dive in confidently. Use the tools and insights you've gained here to build, grow, and sustain a business that survives and thrives. And for those already on this entrepreneurial journey, keep pushing the boundaries. Innovate, expand, and don't hesitate to reevaluate your strategies to ensure they meet the ever-changing business landscape.

I invite you to share your journey with me and others embarking on their own LLC adventures. Your experiences, challenges, and victories add invaluable layers to the collective knowledge and support we can offer each other.

Thank you for allowing me to be a part of your entrepreneurial path. Here's to your success, resilience, and the endless possibilities that await your LLC. Let's keep the conversation going, and remember, the world of business is as much about the journeys we share as the destinations we reach. Happy entrepreneuring!

REFERENCES

- *LLC vs. Sole Proprietorship: How to Choose* https://www.nerdwallet.com/article/small-business/llc-vs-sole-proprietorship
- *How to File LLC Articles of Organization - NerdWallet* https://www.nerdwallet.com/article/small-business/articles-organization
- *7 well-known LLC examples from popular companies:* https://www.doola.com/blog/llc-examples/
- *S Corp vs C Corp - Differences & Benefits* | Wolters Kluwer https://www.wolterskluwer.com/en/expert-insights/s-corp-vs-c-corp-differences-benefits#:~:
- *50-State Guide to Forming an LLC* https://www.nolo.com/legal-encyclopedia/form-llc-in-your-state-31019.html
- *5 Factors to Consider When Choosing a Registered Agent* https://www.harborcompliance.com/blog/5-factors-to-consider-when-choosing-a-registered-agent/
- *How to draft an LLC operating agreement:* https://www.legalzoom.com/articles/how-to-draft-an-llc-operating-agreement
- *undefined* undefined
- *Accounting for LLC: Basics, Best Practices & Tax Obligations* https://profitlineusa.com/accounting-for-llc-basics-best-practices-and-tax-obligations/
- *Best Accounting Software for Small Businesses of June 2024* https://www.nerdwallet.com/best/small-business/accounting-software
- *LLC pass-through taxation: What small business owners need to know* https://www.wolterskluwer.com/en/expert-insights/llc-pass-through-taxation-what-small-business-owners-need-to-know
- *Open a business bank account* https://www.sba.gov/business-guide/launch-your-business/open-business-bank-account
- *Your LLC Annual Report and Tax Filing Requirements* | Nolo https://www.nolo.com/legal-encyclopedia/your-llc-annual-report-filing-requirements.html
- *What Insurance Do You Need for a Small Business?* https://www.thehartford.com/small-business-insurance/what-insurance-do-you-need-for-small-business

- *How to protect your personal assets as an LLC owner* https://www.legalzoom.com/articles/llc-asset-protection-how-to-protect-your-personal-assets-as-an-llc-owner
- *Why Your LLC, Not You, Should Own Your Intellectual ...* https://www.thebrownefirm.com/why-your-llc-not-you-should-own-your-intellectual-property/
- *LLC Good Governance: Top 4 Best Practices* https://www.enterpriseesquire.com/blog/llc-governance-best-practices
- *Can LLCs Have Employees?* https://www.investopedia.com/ask/answers/112315/can-llcs-have-employees.asp
- *How to Create a Strong Brand Identity - Tailor Brands* https://www.tailorbrands.com/blog/create-brand-identity
- *Scalable Business Models: A Small Business Guide (2023)* https://www.shopify.com/blog/scalable-business-models-1
- *How are LLCs taxed? LLC tax benefits and ways to reduce ...* https://tax.thomsonreuters.com/blog/how-are-llcs-taxed-llc-tax-benefits-and-tips-to-reduce-taxes/
- *9 Best Payroll Services For Small Business Of 2024* https://www.forbes.com/advisor/business/software/best-payroll-services/
- *16 Tips to Avoid a Tax Audit of Your Small Business Return* https://www.business.com/articles/16-tips-to-avoid-a-tax-audit-of-your-small-business-return/
- *10 Benefits Of Cloud-based Accounting Software For Small ...* https://thrivecfo.co.za/cloud-based-accounting-software-for-small-businesses/
- *How To Resolve Member Disputes In LLCs: A Guide* https://thejacobslaw.com/how-to-resolve-member-disputes-in-llcs/
- *Restoring Your Small Business to Good Standing* https://www.wolterskluwer.com/en/expert-insights/reinstatement-restoring-your-small-business-to-good-standing
- *20 Solutions For Companies In Financial Crisis* https://www.forbes.com/sites/forbesfinancecouncil/2023/07/19/20-solutions-for-companies-in-financial-crisis/
- *How to Plan for Exiting an LLC* https://www.incnow.com/blog/2018/09/25/llc-member-exit-strategy/
- *20 Best Business Management Software of 2024* https://peoplemanagingpeople.com/tools/best-business-management-software/

- *How to Build Your Social Media Marketing Strategy* https://sproutsocial.com/insights/social-media-marketing-strategy/
- *Strengthen your cybersecurity* | U.S. Small Business ... https://www.sba.gov/business-guide/manage-your-business/strengthen-your-cybersecurity
- *How Small Businesses And Entrepreneurs Can Benefit* ... https://www.forbes.com/sites/elijahclark/2023/11/30/how-small-businesses-and-entrepreneurs-can-benefit-from-ai/
- *Strategies on how to successfully grow your LLC business* https://www.wolterskluwer.com/en/expert-insights/small-business-growth-strategies-for-your-llc
- *Common LLC Legal Mistakes* | Portland, Oregon lawyer https://www.nwcorporatelaw.com/common-llc-legal-mistakes/
- *4 Important LLC Tax Benefits In 2024 - Business* https://www.forbes.com/advisor/business/llc-tax-benefits/
- *Using a Family LLC for Estate Planning* https://www.nolo.com/legal-encyclopedia/family-llc-for-estate-planning.html
- *International Market Research and Feasibility Studies* https://tradecouncil.org/international-market-research-and-feasibility-studies/
- *9 Strategies for Protecting Your Intellectual Property* https://ttconsultants.com/beyond-the-patent-9-unconventional-strategies-for-protecting-your-intellectual-property/
- *Retirement Plans for Self-Employed People* https://www.irs.gov/retirement-plans/retirement-plans-for-self-employed-people
- *5 Obstacles to Internationalization: Navigating Legal and* ... https://gedeth.com/blog/2023/11/02/5-obstacles-to-internationalization-navigating-legal-and-regulatory-challenges-for-your-global-expansion/
- (2022). *Questions on evaluation in the artistic field.* https://core.ac.uk/download/567635330.pdf
- "15 Impactful Knowledge-Sharing Quotes For Your Team!" Bit Blog. Last modified August 21, 2023. https://blog.bit.ai/knowledge-sharing-quotes/